Frommer's

Dublin
day BY day®
3rd Edition

by Jack Jewers

CALGARY PUBLIC LIBRARY

NOV 2016

Contents

Published by:

Frommer Media LLC

Copyright © 2017 by Frommer Media LLC. All rights reserved. No part of this publication may be reproduced, stored in a retrieval system, or transmitted in any form or by any means, electronic, mechanical, photocopying, recording, scanning or otherwise, except as permitted under Sections 107 or 108 of the 1976 United States Copyright Act, without the prior written permission of the Publisher. Requests to the Publisher for permission should be addressed to support@frommermedia.com.

Frommer's is a trademark or registered trademark of Arthur Frommer. Frommer Media LLC is not associated with any product or vendor mentioned in this book.

ISBN 978-1-62887-292-7 (paper), 978-1-62887-293-4 (e-book)

Editorial Director: Pauline Frommer
Editor: Alexis Lipsitz Flippin
Production Editor: Heather Wilcox
Photo Editor: Meghan Lamb
Cartographer: Roberta Stockwell
Compositor: Heather Pope
Indexer: Maro RioFrancos

Front cover photos, left to right: Ha'penny Bridge, © Tourism Ireland/Brian Morrison; Trinity College, © David Soanes; seafood platter at a Dublin pub, © Fáilte Ireland/Rob Durston

Back cover photo: Dubhlinn Garden at Chester Beatty Library, Dublin, © Fáilte Ireland/Rob Durston

For information on our other products and services, please go to Frommers.com.

Frommer's also publishes its books in a variety of electronic formats. Some content that appears in print may not be available in electronic formats.

Manufactured in China

5 4 3 2 1

About This Guide

Organizing your time. That's what this guide is all about.

Other guides give you long lists of things to see and do and then expect you to fit the pieces together. The Day by Day guides are different. These guides tell you the best of everything, and then they show you how to see it in the smartest, most time-efficient way. Our authors have designed detailed itineraries organized by time, neighborhood, or special interest. And each tour comes with a bulleted map that takes you from stop to stop.

Hoping to tour the best in Georgian architecture, stroll down Grafton Street, or taste your way through gourmet Dublin? Planning a walk through Trinity College, or plotting a day of fun-filled activities with the kids? Whatever your interest or schedule, the Day by Days give you the smartest routes to follow. Not only do we take you to the top attractions, hotels, and restaurants, but we also help you access those special moments that locals get to experience—those "finds" that turn tourists into travelers.

The Day by Days are also your top choice if you're looking for one complete guide for all your travel needs. The best hotels and restaurants for every budget, the greatest shopping values, the wildest nightlife—it's all here.

Why should you trust our judgment? Because our authors personally visit each place they write about. They're an independent lot who say what they think and would never include places they wouldn't recommend to their best friends. They're also open to suggestions from readers. If you'd like to contact them, please send your comments our way at feedback@frommers.com, and we'll pass them on.

Enjoy your Day by Day guide—the most helpful travel companion you can buy. And have the trip of a lifetime.

About the Author

Jack Jewers has written about Ireland for Frommer's since 2006. Born and raised in England, he loved listening to his great-aunt's tales about life in Dublin during the civil war. Jack proposed to his Irish-American wife at a spa on the Ring of Kerry.

An Additional Note

Please be advised that travel information is subject to change at any time—and this is especially true of prices. We therefore suggest that you write or call ahead for confirmation when making your travel plans. The authors, editors, and publisher cannot be held responsible for the experiences of readers while traveling. Your safety is important to us, however, so we encourage you to stay alert and be aware of your surroundings.

Star Ratings, Icons & Abbreviations

Every hotel, restaurant, and attraction listing in this guide has been ranked for quality, value, service, amenities, and special features using a **star-rating system.** Hotels, restaurants, attractions, shopping, and nightlife are rated on a scale of zero stars (recommended) to three stars (exceptional). In addition to the star-rating system, we also use a **kids icon** to point out the best bets for families. Within each tour, we recommend cafes, bars, or restaurants where you can take a break. Each of these stops appears in a shaded box marked with a coffee-cup-shaped bullet ☕.

The following **abbreviations** are used for credit cards:

AE	American Express	DISC	Discover	V	Visa
DC	Diners Club	MC	MasterCard		

Frommers.com

Now that you have this guidebook to help you plan a great trip, visit our website at **www.frommers.com** for additional travel information on more than 4,000 destinations. We update features regularly to give you instant access to the most current trip-planning information available. At Frommers.com, you'll find scoops on the best airfares, lodging rates, and car rental bargains. You can even book your travel online through our reliable travel booking partners. Other popular features include:

- Online updates of our most popular guidebooks

- Vacation sweepstakes and contest giveaways

- Newsletters highlighting the hottest travel trends

- Online travel message boards with featured travel discussions

A Note on Prices

In the "Take a Break" (☕) and "Best Bets" sections of this book, we have used a system of dollar signs to show a range of costs for 1 night in a hotel (the price of a double-occupancy room) or the cost of an entree at a restaurant. Use the following table to decipher the dollar signs:

Cost	Hotels	Restaurants
$	under $100	under $10
$$	$100–$200	$10–$20
$$$	$200–$300	$20–$30
$$$$	$300–$400	$30–$40
$$$$$	over $400	over $40

How to Contact Us

In researching this book, we discovered many wonderful places—hotels, restaurants, shops, and more. We're sure you'll find others. Please tell us about them, so we can share the information with your fellow travelers in upcoming editions. If you were disappointed with a recommendation, we'd love to know that, too. Please write to: Contact@FrommerMedia.com

10 Favorite Moments

10 Favorite Moments

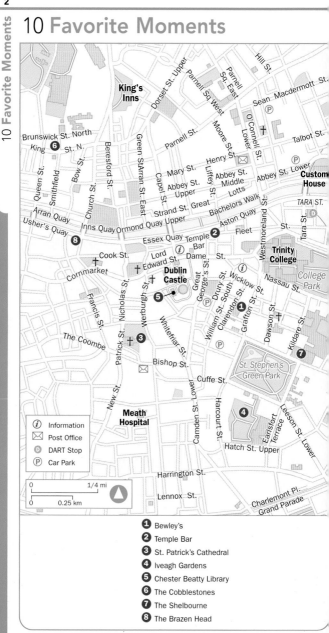

1. Bewley's
2. Temple Bar
3. St. Patrick's Cathedral
4. Iveagh Gardens
5. Chester Beatty Library
6. The Cobblestones
7. The Shelbourne
8. The Brazen Head

Previous page: Temple Bar.

For such an ancient town, Dublin does a pretty good job of not showing its age. This is a town where you'll find history at every turn, whether it be down winding Georgian alleyways, in the crypts of ancient Medieval churches, or even in the timeworn snugs of its storied old pubs. Much about Dublin has changed enormously over the past couple of decades, and it now feels as much like a cosmopolitan European city as it does merely the capital of Ireland. Entire districts have been transformed almost out of recognition for anybody who might have visited here, say, 20 or 30 years ago. But some things don't change. Many of these favorite moments will feel as permanent for lovers of this captivating old town as they ever were.

❶ **People-watching from the balcony at Bewley's.** The human traffic of busy Grafton Street flows past the tiny balcony at this beloved café, immortalized in literature and a favored hangout of Dubliners for a century. Stopping here for coffee and cake is still a quintessential Dublin experience. *See p 93.*

❷ **Walking through Temple Bar.** Yes, it's touristy, yes, it's loud, and yes, it's the kind of place where people in giant leprechaun costumes hustle for change in return for photos…. But the energy of Temple Bar is electrifying. Its restaurants and bars buzz with life, its galleries and cultural centers overflow with innovation. *See p 62.*

❸ **Watching the sunlight inside St. Patrick's Cathedral.** Late afternoon usually means Evensong's organ rehearsals in this historic cathedral. As the sun starts to dip, watch the glowing colors on the walls as the light shines through the stained-glass windows. *See p 8.*

❹ **Sauntering through wooded walks at Iveagh Gardens.** So close to busy St. Stephen's Green and yet a world away, this secluded Victorian garden has a cascade, armless statues, a rosarium, and shady woods—all made for solitary afternoons. *See p 92.*

❺ **Gaping at the manuscripts in the Chester Beatty Library.** Not all that well known even among Dubliners, the Chester Beatty is quite simply the best small museum we've ever been to in Ireland. Why stand in long lines to see a couple of pages from the Book of Kells when this is here—and for free? *See p 39.*

❻ **Catching a traditional music session at the Cobblestones.** You won't have to look far at all to find live music in Dublin's myriad fine pubs—but if it's true authenticity you're after, you need to know

View of Grafton Street from Bewley's.

St. Patrick's Cathedral.

where to go. And this, for our money, is the cream of the crop. *See p 118.*

7 Taking afternoon tea at the Shelbourne. You don't have to be an overnight guest to sink into a huge leather armchair at this classic Dublin hotel and demolish a tower of cakes and daintily trimmed sandwiches. If you're in the mood for a history fix afterward, sneak upstairs to find room no. 112. This is where the Irish Constitution was written in 1922. If nobody has booked the room—and the concierge is in a good mood—you might even get to peek inside. *See p 146.*

8 Listening to a master storyteller spin a yarn. The last few years have seen a resurgence in the age-old art of storytelling, with a new generation embracing this captivatingly simple art form. There's a magic about it that feels almost primal. **An Evening of Food, Folklore and Fairies** is one of the most unexpectedly fun nights out Dublin has to offer—and appropriately enough it's held in what might be Ireland's oldest pub. If you believe the story. *See p 133.*

9 Deciding who serves the best pint of Guinness. Guinness might be available the world over, but it really does taste better over here. (Throw shade on anyone who tells you it's because they use water from the Liffey—Irish Guinness is unpasteurized, unlike the kind they export.) So where's it to be? Doheny and Nesbitt? The Long Hall? Grogan's Castle? Hard to tell, but it's always a mouthwatering moment watching the pint being pulled slowly and then settling, ready to be sunk. *See p 117.*

10 Enjoying the foodie culture. During the "Celtic Tiger" boom years of the 1990s and early 2000s, Dublin developed a gastronomic scene quite unlike anything it had experienced before, with a host of cutting-edge restaurants taking the city by storm. Many are still here, but the current trend towards a rediscovery (and reinvention) of traditional Irish flavors is even more appealing. Places like **Gallagher's Boxty House** in Temple Bar are embracing Ireland's traditional food heritage afresh for a new generation. *See p 99.* ●

View of Dubhlinn Garden and city from the roof garden at Chester Beatty.

1

The Best
Full-Day Tours

The Best **in** One Day

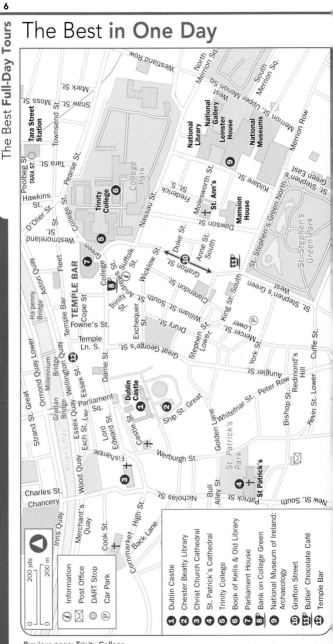

Tara Street Station

TARA ST.

National Library

National Gallery

Leinster House

National Museums ⑨

Trinity College ⑥

College Park

St. Ann's

Mansion House

St. Stephen's Green Park

TEMPLE BAR ⑦

⑤

⑧ ①

🕮 ⑩

Dublin Castle ①

② ⑫

③ ✝

St Patrick's ④ ✝

St Patrick's Park

0   200 yds
0   200 m

ℹ Information
⊠ Post Office
◉ DART Stop
Ⓟ Car Park

① Dublin Castle
② Chester Beatty Library
③ Christ Church Cathedral
④ St. Patrick's Cathedral
⑤ Trinity College
⑥ Book of Kells & Old Library
⑦ Parliament House
⑧ Bank on College Green
⑨ National Museum of Ireland: Archaeology
⑩ Grafton Street
🕮 Butler' Chocolate Café
⑫ Temple Bar

Previous page: Trinity College.

This full day kicks off with some of Dublin's most famous landmarks. You might not have the chance to see everything, but the beauty of compact Dublin is that you'll probably be retracing your steps on another day. It's a city for walking, with scant need for public transport, so don your comfortable shoes—and waterproofs. START: **all cross-city buses to O'Connell St. LUAS: Abbey St.**

① ★ **Dublin Castle.** It's fair to say that this is not among Ireland's most impressive castles, but it's a good place nonetheless to anchor yourself as you begin to explore the capital. The epicenter of British power in Ireland from the 1200s until the 1920s, Dublin Castle is now a government building. You can wander the peaceful courtyard grounds for free. Guided tours of the interior allow you to see the majestic State Apartments, Treasury, and the Gothic-style Chapel Royal. ⏱ *1 hr. Dame St. www.heri tageireland.ie.* ☎ *01-645 8813. Free admission to grounds; tour €6.70 adults, €5.70 seniors, €3.20 students and children (11 & under). Guided tour €8.50 adults, €7.50 seniors, €4 students & children. Mon–Sat 9:45am–4:45pm; Sun & public holidays noon–4:45pm. Luas: Jervis. Bus: inc. 13, 37, 39.*

② ★★★ **Chester Beatty Library.** On the grounds of Dublin Castle lies this wonderful small museum, unassuming enough that even many Dublin residents have never heard of it. And yet within lies a dazzling collection of early

Chester Beatty Library.

religious texts and other priceless artifacts. Highlights include breath-taking illuminated gospels; impeccable 15th-century Quarans and Quaranic scrolls from the 8th and 9th centuries; and sacred Buddhist texts from Burma and Tibet. If there's a better museum of this size in Ireland, we have yet to find it. ⏱ *1 hr. Dame St. www.cbl.ie.* ☎ *01/407-0750. Free admission. Mon–Fri 10am–5pm; Sat 11am–5pm; Sun 1pm–5pm. Luas: Jervis. Bus: inc. 13, 37, 39.*

The 12th-century crypt at Christ Church Cathedral.

❸ ★★ Christ Church Cathedral. One of Dublin's two great cathedrals, Christ Church was started in 1038. In 1171, the original foundation was extended into a cruciform layout and rebuilt in stone by the Norman warrior Strongbow. The present structure dates mainly from a controversial renovation in the late 19th century. Some beautiful stonework and pointed arches survive from the 12th-century structure. The best way to visualize what the Norman building must have looked like is to visit the 12th-century crypt, which was untouched by the restoration. ⏲ 45 min. Christchurch Pl. www. christchurchdublin.ie. ☎ 01/677-8099. Admission €6 adults; €4.50 seniors & students; €2 children € (15 and under); €15 families. Free entry for prayer or services. Apr–Sept Mon–Sat 9am–7pm; Sun 12:30–2:30pm & 4:30–6pm. Mar & Oct Mon–Sat 9am–6pm; Sun 12:30–2:30pm & 4:30–6pm. Nov–Feb Mon–Sat 9am–5pm; Sun 12:30–2:30pm. Bus: inc. 37, 39, 49.

❹ ★★ St. Patrick's Cathedral. A leisurely 10-minute walk down the hill from Christ Church will bring you to Dublin's other great cathedral—and its most famous. Most of what you can see dates from the 14th century, but religious buildings stood here nearly a thousand years before that. It is mainly early English in style, with a square medieval tower that houses the largest ringing peal bells in Ireland, as well as an 18th-century spire. ⏲ 45 min. St. Patrick's Close. www. stpatrickscathedral.ie. ☎ 01/453-9472. Admission €6 adults; €5 seniors & students; €3 children; €15 families. Mar–Oct Mon–Fri 9:30am–5pm; Sat 9am–6pm; Sun 9–10:30am, 12:30–2:30pm & 4:30–6pm. Nov–Feb Mon–Fri 9:30am–5pm; Sat 9am–5pm; Sun 9am–10:30am & 12:30–2:30pm. Bus: inc. 49, 77, 150.

❺ ★★ Trinity College. Ireland's oldest university, founded in 1592 by Queen Elizabeth I, is an oasis of lawns, cobbled paths, and myriad architectural styles ranging from the 1700s to the 1900s. Walk through the main entrance flanked by the two statues of old boys **Oliver Goldsmith** (1728–74) and **Edmund Burke** (1729–97) to the graceful white Campanile, a famous Dublin landmark. Explore the 16 hectares (40 acres) of grounds, and remember you're pacing the hallowed turf

St. Patrick's Cathedral.

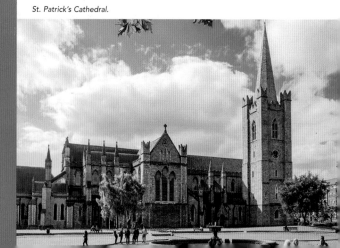

Long Room at Trinity College Library.

of an establishment that educated the likes of Oscar Wilde, Bram Stoker, and Samuel Beckett. The campus is free to walk around, but if you're visiting between May and September, the excellent **Trinity Tours** covers all of the main sights, including its star attraction: the Book of Kells (see below). ⏱ *30 min. See "Special-Interest Tours: Trinity College," p 34.*

⑥ ★★ Book of Kells & Old Library. People tend to have one of two reactions to the Book of Kells. You may find yourself awed by the beautiy of this 1,200-year-old illuminated gospel, which was painstakingly hand-drawn by the monks of Kells Abbey, County Meath. But you might equally wonder whether it's quite worth the cost and effort, which can involve standing in a lengthy queue—especially if you've followed our advice and spent part of the morning at the Chester Beatty Library, which rather makes this pale by comparison. Still, it's a shame to come all this way and miss it. Afterwards, be sure to take the time to visit the college's Harry Potter-esque **Old Library** (included in the same ticket). ⏱ *45 min. The Library*

Building, Trinity College. www.tcd.ie/ visitors/book-of-kells/. ☎ 01/896-2320. Admission €10 adults; €9 seniors, students & children; €20 families. June–Sept Mon–Sat 9am–6pm; Sun 9:30am–6pm. Oct–May Mon–Sat 9:30am–5pm; Sun noon–4:30pm. Last admission 30 min before closing. DART: Pearse St., Connolly St. Luas: Lower Abbey St., St. Stephen's Green. Bus (Nassau St. entrance) inc. 25X, 32X, 33X.

⑦ ★ Parliament House. Adjacent to Trinity College, this grand colonnaded building might look somewhat familiar—it was supposedly the model for the U.S. Capitol Building in Washington, D.C. Today, somewhat disappointingly, it's owned by the Bank of Ireland; however you can see parts of the grand interior, including 18th-century tapestries. The bank employs porters who are always on hand to help field inquiries about the building, and will even show you around some more of the rooms if you ask nicely. ⏱ *15 min. College Green.* ☎ *01/671-1488. Free admission. Mon–Wed, Fri 10am–4pm; Thurs 10am–5pm. DART: Tara Street. LUAS: St. Stephen's Green, Jervis St. Bus: inc. 9, 13, 16.*

Trinity College.

8 ★★ **Bank on College Green.** Directly opposite Trinity College, this beautiful Victorian bank building is one of the city's finest pubs. It also serves excellent food—so where better for a restorative lunch? *20 College Green.* ☎ *01-677 0677. $$.*

9 ★★★ **National Museum of Ireland: Archaeology.** This sprawling museum is packed with objects dating as far back as the Stone Age. Highlights include an extraordinary hoard of Viking treasure; precious early Christian artifacts; and *objets d'art* from the Middle Ages up to the 19th century. One of three sites in Dublin that collectively make up the National Museum, this is perhaps the most essential, and deserves a couple of hours to do properly. ⏱ *2 hr. Kildare St. www.museum.ie.* ☎ *01/677-7444. Free admission. Tues–Sat 10am–5pm; Sun 2–5pm. Bus: inc. 7B, 10, 11.*

10 ★★ **Grafton Street.** A walk down Dublin's most fashionable street is a great way of rounding off your first day. Depending on whether you're more in the mood to shop than to wander, you may want to swap this with the National Museum, although we prefer to

take Dublin first-timers for a late afternoon stroll down the glittering boulevard, which is lined with fashionable boutiques and big chain stores. Among the most famous is the department store **Brown Thomas** (☎ 01/605-6666), at no. 88, which has been here since 1848. Grafton Street's southern end, at the entrance to St. Stephen's Green, is dominated by the grand **Royal Fusiliers' Arch.** Midway down, stop at **Bewley's** (see p 93), since 1840 a famous coffee haven and little changed since then. Grafton Street is also the unofficial venue for myriad buskers, from Romanian accordionists to Irish fiddlers and wannabe rock stars—the best ones usually playing early evening or at night. ⏱ *30 min. All buses to St. Stephen's Green.*

11 ★★ **Butler's Chocolate Café.** These Dublin chocolatiers have been making sumptuous treats in the city since 1932. You'll find a branch of their "Chocolate Café" at the St. Stephen's Green end of Grafton Street and another on nearby Chatham Street. Stop here for a pick-me-up. The white hot chocolate is life-changing. *51 Grafton St.* ☎ *01-616/7004 & 9 Chatham St.* ☎ *01-672 6333. $.*

Grafton Street.

Dublin Pass

If you're planning a lot of sightseeing in Dublin, the tourism board would like you to consider purchasing its **Dublin Pass,** which offers free admission to most of the city's major sights, as well as free travel from the airport on the AirCoach shuttle, and discounts at a number of shops, bars, and restaurants. Unfortunately, the pass is a bit pricey, given that so many of Dublin's sights are free. So our advice is this: If you're leaning heavy on the sightseeing, buy the pass, but plan carefully how best to use it. For example, consider buying a pass good for 1 or 2 days, and then see all of the city's most expensive sights (the Guinness Storehouse, Kilmainham Gaol, and so forth) on those days. On the other days of your trip, you can devote your time to the museums, parks, and galleries that charge no entrance fee. An adult pass costs €41 for 1 day, €63 for 2 days, €73 for 3 days, and €107 for 6 days. A child's pass costs €23 for 1 day, €37 for 2 days, €44 for 3 days, and €56 for 6 days. You can purchase a pass at any Dublin Tourism office or online at **www. dublinpass.ie**. There are sometimes advance-purchase discounts.

⓬ ★★ **Temple Bar.** If you're feeling sleepy after such a long day, an evening here is sure to wake you up. Temple Bar is an artsy, cultured district full of trendy shops and modern art galleries. But such refinement gives way to an altogether more raucous atmosphere at night. With its myriad selection of pubs, bars, and hip clubs, this is definitely where it's at in Dublin after dark. ① *2 hr. (or however long you can take it!).*

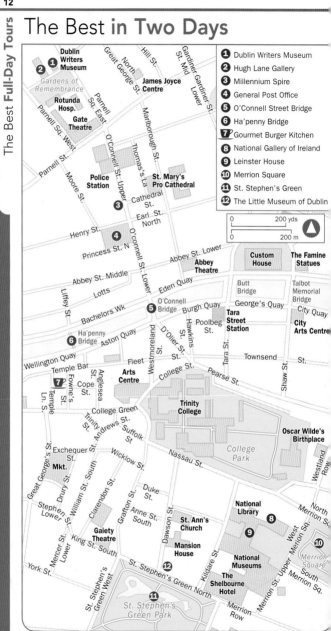

The Best in Two Days

1. Dublin Writers Museum
2. Hugh Lane Gallery
3. Millennium Spire
4. General Post Office
5. O'Connell Street Bridge
6. Ha'penny Bridge
7. Gourmet Burger Kitchen
8. National Gallery of Ireland
9. Leinster House
10. Merrion Square
11. St. Stephen's Green
12. The Little Museum of Dublin

After a full first day, the pace doesn't slow, although you can choose whether it's an in-depth visit or a quick look at many of these attractions. We delve further into Dublin's history today, taking in some more of its most famous landmarks—and getting better acquainted with some of the great artists and writers who have called this place home. START: Bus 4, 5, 7 & 45 to Merrion Square.

❶ ★★ Dublin Writers Museum.

You may have heard that Ireland has produced a good writer or two, and this museum on the north side of the city is a wonderful place for lovers of Irish literature to explore. Highlights include the personal effects of **James Joyce, Oscar Wilde,** and other greats of the canon. Those already familiar with the work of the writers featured here will come away with a richer understanding of their genius. Meanwhile, those seeking an introduction will want to allow extra time to lose themselves in the museum's excellent bookshop. The museum is in Parnell Square, about a 10-minute walk uphill from the bottom of O'Connell Street. ⓧ 1 hr. 18 Parnell Sq. www.writersmuseum.com. ☎ 01/872-2077. Admission €7.50 adults; €6.50 seniors & students; €5 children; €18 families. Mon–Sat 10am–5pm; Sun 11am–5pm. Bus: inc. 1, 2, 8.

❷ ★★ Hugh Lane Gallery.

This small art gallery punches above its weight with a strong collection of Impressionist works. Highlights of the collection include Degas's *Sur la Plage* and Manet's *La Musique aux Tuileries*. There are also sculptures by Rodin, a stunning collection of Arts and Crafts stained glass by Dublin-born artist Harry Clarke (don't miss his masterpiece, *The Eve of St. Agnes*), and numerous works by modern Irish artists. One room holds the maddeningly cluttered studio of the Irish painter Francis Bacon. The gallery purchased the London studio and moved it to Dublin, where it has been reconstructed behind glass. Everything was moved—right down to the dust. It's an excellent, compact art museum, and a great place to spend an hour or so. ⓧ 1 hr. Parnell Sq. North. www.hughlane.ie. ☎ 01/222-5550. Free admission. Tues–Thurs 10am–6pm; Fri–Sat 10am–5pm; Sun 11am–5pm. Closed Mon. Bus: inc. 1, 2, 8.

Dublin Writers Museum.

❸ ★ Millennium Spire. Walk down O'Connell Street from Parnell Square, and you really can't fail to notice this controversial monument. Dubliners have a love-hate relationship with the enormous spire, which was completed in 2003—3 years late—to commemorate the Millennium. The 120m (395-ft.) high stainless steel spire, 3m (10 ft.) wide at the base and tapering to 15cm (6 in.) at the top, is the tallest city-center structure and impossible to miss. We'd argue that the much-maligned monument has aged surprisingly well, however; the way that it changes color according to the time of day is particularly clever (metallic blue at sunrise and sunset; shiny gray in the day; and black at night with tiny lights on the upper sections). In common with Dublin tradition, locals have their own, dry nicknames for the monument; among the more printable is "the Stiletto in the Ghetto." ⏱ *2 min. Bus: All buses to O'Connell St.*

❹ ★ General Post Office. O'Connell Street—though hardly the most attractive of Dublin's main thoroughfares—holds a vital place in Ireland's national psyche. This was where some of the fiercest fighting took place during the War of Independence in the early 1920s. Most iconic of all is the Post Office building—also known as the GPO—which became the headquarters of the rebels during the Easter Rising of 1916. (The Declaration of Independence was read out on the front steps.) Designed by Francis Johnston and built in 1814, its distinctive Doric columns span the five central bays, with John Smyth's statues of Fidelity, Hibernia, and Mercury above the portico. It's still a working post office, and the building's iconic status is the main attraction—but the modest **Letters, Lives and Liberty Museum** inside

O'Connell Bridge with O'Connell Street and the Spire in the background.

is worth a look if you want to learn more. *See also p 47.* ⏱ *5 min. An Post, O'Connell St. www.anpost.ie.* ☎ *01/705-8833. Free admission. Counters open Mon–Sat 8:30am–6pm.*

❺ ★ O'Connell Street Bridge. Stand on the north side of O'Connell Bridge by the statue of **Daniel O'Connell**, and you're in what many Dubliners believe is the very heart of the city. The man himself, cast impressively in bronze (see p 47, **❽**), was a politician and patriot in the 1800s and the first Catholic to enter the House of Commons. Edge past the photo-snapping tourists and look for the bullet holes in the angels ringing the base of the statue. The bridge is unique in Europe: A multi-lane traffic highway, it is even wider than it is long. ⏱ *5 min. Bus: All cross-city buses.*

❻ ★ Ha'penny Bridge. Though the O'Connell Street Bridge gets the fancy statues, this is the path you want to take across the River Liffey. Built in 1816, and one of the earliest cast-iron bridges in Europe, the graceful, pedestrian-only Ha'penny Bridge (pronounced

Hay-penny) is the still the most attractive of Dublin's bridges. Officially named the Liffey Bridge, it's universally known by the toll it once charged to cross it: half a penny. (Local lore would have it that the charge was to discourage the "hoi polloi" of the Northside away from venturing to the more cultured Southside.) The turnstiles were removed in 1919 when passage was made free. In recent years it became traditional for couples to leave padlocks latched onto the bridge, with their names inscribed, before throwing the keys into the water. Dublin's city government now forbids the practice, seeing them more as an eyesore than a symbol of eternal love. ⏰ *10 min. Bus: All buses to O'Connell St. LUAS: Abbey St.*

7 ★★ **Gourmet Burger Kitchen.** A short walk from the Temple Bar end of the Ha'Penny Bridge, this upscale but relaxed burger joint is great for a quick and tasty lunch. *Temple Bar Sq.* ☎ *01/670-8343. $$.*

8 ★★ **National Gallery of Ireland.** George Bernard Shaw loved this place so much that he left it one-third of his royalties in perpetuity after he died. He saw it as paying a debt, so important was the gallery to his education. It is still a place to wander, wonder, and just be in thrall to so much beautiful art. Highlights of the permanent collection include paintings by Caravaggio, Gainsborough, Rubens, Goya, Rembrandt, Monet, and Picasso. The Irish national portrait collection is housed in one wing, while another area is devoted to the career of Jack B. Yeats (brother of W. B. Yeats), an Irish painter of some note. Major exhibitions change regularly, and the subjects are often more imaginative than just the usual run of retrospectives and national landscapes (although those appear too); recent shows have included an intriguing exhibition of mixed-media sculpture, re-creating images of Irish migration in the 18th and 19th centuries. In keeping with the "art for all" ethos that so enamored Bernard Shaw, entry to the permanent collection is free. ⏰ *2 hr. Merrion Sq. West. www.nationalgallery.ie.* ☎ *01/661-5133. Free admission. Mon–Wed, Fri–Sat 9:30am–5:30pm; Thurs 9:30am–8:30pm; Sun 11am–5:30pm; public holidays 10am–5:30pm. DART: Pearse. Luas: St. Stephen's Green, Grafton St. Bus: inc. 4, 5, 7.*

9 ★ **Leinster House.** Walk up Merrion Square South and peek through the sturdy railings to see the two houses of the National Parliament: the **Dáil** (House of Deputies) and **Seanad** (Senate). Built in 1745 as the town house of the Earl of Kildare, who later became the Duke of Leinster, this is said to be a prototype for the U.S. White House (which was built by Dublin-educated architect James Hoban). At the time, the area was undeveloped

National Gallery of Ireland.

and known rather disparagingly as "the lands of tib and tom." The Earl was advised against building a town house in the "country." But he had the last laugh when 2 decades later this became the most fashionable part of town. When the Dáil is not in session, tickets are available for guided tours, three times a day, on Mondays and Fridays. You don't have to book a spot, but numbers are strictly limited. To reserve tickets, the events desk prefers an e-mail (event.desk@oireachtas.ie; include your full name, address, and telephone number), or you can call ☎ 1890/252-4551. *Note:* You need to bring photo I.D. (such as a driver's license or passport) to gain admission, and you shouldn't bring large or bulky bags. ⏱ *tour 40 min. Kildare St. & Merrion Sq. www. oireachtas.ie.* ☎ *01-619 3186. Free admission. Entry by tour only, Mon & Fri 10:30am, 2:30, 3:30pm. (Additional tours when Dáil & Seanad in session: Tues & Wed 7pm, 8pm.) Bus: inc. 4, 5, 10.*

⑩ ★ **Merrion Square.** One of Dublin's most elegant Georgian squares, this was considered—and still is—the most noble part of the city. Wander through the neat lawns and trees of its interior, **Archbishop Ryan Park,** and look out for the sculpture of **Oscar Wilde** reclining and gazing wistfully towards his childhood home, 1 Merrion Square (now the American University). Three sides of the square are lined with beautifully preserved Georgian houses, including **Number Twenty Nine house museum** (see below). The square's railings are the venue for the weekend **Art Market,** busy in summer. ⏱ *20 min. Bus: inc. 7, 10, 45.*

⑪ ★★ **St. Stephen's Green.** This lovely city center park is filled with public art, and there always seems to be something new and imaginative hidden amid its leafy walkways. Among them is a beautiful statue commemorating the Irish rebel Wolfe Tone (beside an affecting monument to the Great Famine) and a garden of scented plants for blind visitors. ⏱ *30 min. Luas: St. Stephen's Green. Bus: inc. 20B, 32X, 33X.*

⑫ ★★ **The Little Musem of Dublin.** This endearing museum was built up thanks to the donations of ordinary Dubliners, who together assembled an extraordinary chronicle of everyday life in the capital in the 20th century.

Artists display their work in Merrion Square.

Items on display here include photographs, household items, newspapers, and assorted curios. The helpful guides are great at putting everything into context, particularly for kids. ⏱ *1 hr. 15 St. Stephen's Green. www.littlemuseum.ie. ☎ 01/661-1000. Admission €7 adults; €5.50 seniors; €4.50 students & children; €14 families. Deluxe ticket (includes private guided tour) €12. Daily 9:30am–5pm (open until 8pm Thurs). Luas: St. Stephen's Green. Bus: inc. 15X, 32X, 39X.*

The Little Museum of Dublin.

The Best **in Three Days**

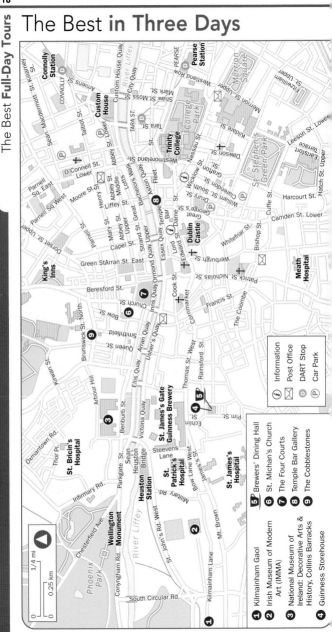

❶ Kilmainham Gaol
❷ Irish Museum of Modern Art (IMMA)
❸ National Museum of Ireland: Decorative Arts & History, Collins Barracks
❹ Guinness Storehouse
❺ Brewers' Dining Hall
❻ St. Michan's Church
❼ The Four Courts
❽ Temple Bar Gallery
❾ The Cobblestones

ⓘ Information
⊠ Post Office
Ⓓ DART Stop
Ⓟ Car Park

It's time to venture a little farther out of the center this morning, as you get to know some of the sights of Smithfield, on the eastern side of the city. Then it's back to Temple Bar in the afternoon, before rounding off the day at one of the city's best venues for authentic, traditional live music. START: **Bus: 3, 11, 16 or 46A from O'Connell Street to Croke Park.**

❶ ★★★ Kilmainham Gaol. For nearly 130 years this was one of the most notorious prisons in Ireland. In addition to a grim roll call of the criminally insane, Kilmainham's inmates counted several prominent Irish revolutionaries among their number. These included Patrick Pearse, who led the Easter Rising of 1916 (and was executed here just weeks later), and Eamon de Valera, who eventually wound up as president of Ireland. Walking through the restored building, with its Victorian cells and austere exercise yard, is a powerful experience. The accompanying exhibition does an outstanding job of putting all this history into context. ⏱ *2 hr. Inchicore Rd. www.heritageireland.ie/en/Dublin/KilmainhamGaol.* ☎ *01/453-5984. Admission €6 adults; €4 seniors; €2 students & children; €14 families. Apr–Sept daily 9:30am–6pm; Oct–Mar Mon–Sat 9:30am–5:30pm, Sun 10am–6pm. Last admission 1 hr. before closing. Luas: Suir Road. Bus: inc. 13, 40, 79.*

❷ ★★ Irish Museum of Modern Art. Set in a beautiful 17th-century former hospital building, this small but handsome museum has a strong collection of modern art dating from the 1940s to the present day. Highlights include a striking series of mid-1970s photographs by the Serbian conceptual artist Marina Abramovic; etchings and lithographs by Alice Maher, Louis le Brocquy, and Marcel Duchamp; and the Madden Arnholz Collection, made up of around 2,000 old master prints, including works

by Rembrandt. The beautifully restored grounds are also used as an exhibition space, with a number of changing pieces displayed among the formal lawns and clipped box hedges. ⏱ *1 hr. Royal Hospital, Military Rd., Kilmainham, Dublin 8. www.imma.ie.* ☎ *01/612-9900. Free admission. Tues–Fri 11:30am–5:30pm; Sat 10am–5:30pm; Sun & public holidays noon–5:30pm. Last admission 45 min. before closing. Closed Mon. Luas: Heuston. Bus: inc. 13, 40, 79.*

❸ ★★ National Museum of Ireland: Decorative Arts & History, Collins Barracks. As the name of this branch of the National Museum of Ireland suggests, the collection tells the story of Irish (and world) history through fashion, jewelry, furniture, and other decorative arts, with the bulk of the collection spanning the 1760s to

Entrance to the Irish Museum of Modern Art.

The Gravity Bar at the Guinness Storehouse.

the 1960s. One gallery is devoted to the work of Eileen Gray (1878–1976), an Irish architect and furniture designer who became one of the most important figures of the Modernist movement; another showcases the extraordinary collection of Asian art bequeathed to the Irish nation in the 1930s by Irish-American philanthropist Albert Bender. Set in a converted 18th-century army building, this branch of the National Museum isn't entirely devoted to the arts; eight galleries cover Irish military history from the 16th century to the present day, including a fascinating section about the Easter Rising of 1916. ⏱ *2 hr. Benburb St. www.museum.ie.* ☎ *01/677-7444. Free admission. Tues–Sat 10am–5pm; Sun 2–5pm. Luas: Museum. Rail: Heuston. Bus: 39B, 70N.*

❹ ★ Guinness Storehouse.

Opened in 1759, the Guinness Storehouse is one of the world's most famous breweries, producing the distinctive dark stout that is known and loved the world over. You can explore the Guinness Hopstore, tour a converted 19th-century building housing the World of Guinness Exhibition, and view a film showing how the stout is made; then move on to the Gilroy Gallery, dedicated to the graphic design work of John Gilroy (whose work you will have seen if you've ever been in an Irish pub); and last but not least, stop in at the breathtaking Gravity Bar. Here you can sample a glass of the famous brew in the glass-enclosed bar 61m (200 ft.) above the ground, complete with 360-degree views of the city. ⏱ *90 min. St. James's Gate, off Robert St. www.guinness-storehouse. com.* ☎ *01/408-4800. Admission €20 adults; €16 seniors & students over 18; €13.50 student under 18; €6.50 children 6–12 (children 5 & under free); €46.50 families. Sept–May daily 9:30am–5pm (last admission); July–Aug daily 9:30am–6pm (last admission). Luas: St. James's Hospital. Bus: 123.*

❺ ★★ Brewers' Dining Hall.

Located on the fifth floor of the Guinness Storehouse, this relaxed restaurant serves good, classic Irish cooking. *Guinness Storehouse, St. James's Gate.* ☎ *01/408-4800. $$.*

❻ ★★ St. Michan's Church.

This remarkable 17th-century church was built on the site of a Viking chapel, dating from around 1095. The interior has some intricate 18th-century woodwork and an organ on which Handel is reputed to have first performed his *Messiah*. However, none of this is really what you're here to see—for the crypt holds a fascinating (and creepy) secret. There's something about the atmospheric conditions down here (no one ever quite seems able to tell us what) that makes bodies decompose extremely slowly. Centuries-old mummies are laid out in open coffins, dry and desiccated but in no way looking their age; some even have hair and fingernails. The identities of those interred here have been lost, but they each carry nicknames—the Crusader, the Nun, the Thief—which helps remind us that these were once real people, not just a macabre sideshow. ⏱ *45 min. Church St., Dublin 7.* ☎ *01/872-4154. Admission €5 adults; €4 seniors & students; €3.50 children; €15 families. Crypt: Mid-Mar to Oct Mon–Fri 10am–12:45pm & 2–4:45pm; Sat 10am–12:45pm. Nov to mid-Mar Mon–Fri 12:30–3:30pm; Sat 10am–12:45pm. No crypt tours Sun. Luas: Four Courts, Smithfield. Bus: 51D, 51X.*

7 ★ **The Four Courts.** Home to the Irish legal courts since 1796, this fine 18th-century building is distinguished by its graceful Corinthian columns, massive dome, and exterior statues of Justice, Mercy, Wisdom, and Moses. Badly damaged by the fighting during the civil war of 1922, this building was later artfully restored, although some details, such as the statues of famous Irish lawyers that once adorned the niches of the Round Hall, were lost. Tours are available, but frustratingly only for law students (who must book as part of a group). Otherwise, if you want to see the interior, you can go watch a trial in progress. ⏱ *10 min. Inns Quay. www.courts.ie.* ☎ *01/888-6000. Luas: Four Courts. Bus: inc. 25, 68, 78.*

8 ★★ **Temple Bar Gallery.** It's back across the river to Temple Bar for the last couple of stops on your 3-day tour of the city. This big, rambling art gallery sums up all that is good about Temple Bar. Founded in 1983 in the heart of Dublin's "Left Bank," it's one of the largest studio and gallery complexes of its kind in Europe. It's filled with innovative work by contemporary Irish artists—more than 30 of them, in a variety of disciplines including sculpture, painting, printing, and photography. The colors and creativity are dazzling, and it's run by

The Four Courts.

Tadhg, Méabh & Friends at the Cobblestones.

helpful, friendly people. Only the gallery section is open to the public, but you can make an appointment in advance to view individual artists at work. The Studios host free talks and discussion panels, featuring the great and the good of the Irish arts scene. Call or go online for details. ○ *90 min. 5–9 Temple Bar. www.templebargallery. com.* ☎ *01/671-0073. Free admission. Tues–Sat 11am–6pm. Bus: 26, 37, 39.*

❾ ★★★ The Cobblestones. Dublin is hardly short of memorable pubs to choose from, but this tucked-away gem is one that many visitors pass by. This is a real musician's pub, beloved by locals, and as authentic as they come. Traditional music sessions happen nightly in the main bar, and admission is free. *Sláinte mhaith! 77 N. King St., Smithfield. www.cobblestonepub.ie.* ☎ *01/872-1799. Mon–Thurs 4–11:30pm; Fri–Sat 4pm–12:30am; Sun 1–11pm. Luas: 37, 39, 70.* ●

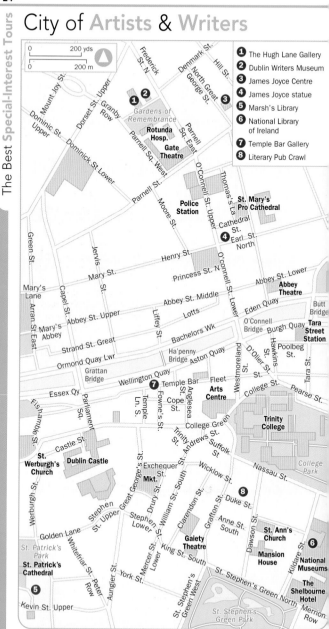

City of Artists & Writers

| 0 | 200 yds |
| 0 | 200 m |

1 The Hugh Lane Gallery
2 Dublin Writers Museum
3 James Joyce Centre
4 James Joyce statue
5 Marsh's Library
6 National Library of Ireland
7 Temple Bar Gallery
8 Literary Pub Crawl

Frederick St. N
Denmark St.
Hill St.
North Great George St.
Mount Joy St.
Dominic St. Upper
Dorset St. Upper
Granby Row
Parnell Sq. East
Gardens of Remembrance
Rotunda Hosp.
Parnell Sq. West
Dominick St. Lower
Gate Theatre
Parnell St.
O'Connell St. Upper
Moore St.
Thomas's La.
St. Mary's Pro Cathedral
Police Station
Cathedral St.
Earl St. North
Green St.
Jervis St.
Henry St.
Princess St. N.
O'Connell St. Lower
Mary's Lane
Mary's Abbey
Capel St.
Abbey St. Upper
Mary St.
Liffey St.
Abbey St. Middle
Lotts
Abbey St. Lower
Abbey Theatre
Eden Quay
Butt Bridge
Arran St. East
Strand St. Great
Bachelors Wk.
O'Connell Bridge
Burgh Quay
Tara Street Station
Ormond Quay Lwr.
Ha'penny Bridge
Aston Quay
Poolbeg St.
Grattan Bridge
Wellington Quay
Westmoreland
D'Olier St.
Hawkins St.
Tara St.
Essex Qy.
Temple Bar
Fleet St.
College St.
Pearse St.
Fishamble St.
Parliament Sq.
Temple Ln. S.
Fownes's St.
Cope St.
Anglesea St.
Arts Centre
Trinity St.
College Green
St. Andrews St.
Suffolk St.
Trinity College
Castle St.
St. Werburgh's Church
Dublin Castle
Exchequer St.
Wicklow St.
Nassau St.
College Park
Werburgh St.
Great George's St. Upper
Mkt.
Drury St.
William St. South
Clarendon St.
Duke St.
Anne St. South
St. Ann's Church
Golden Lane
Stephen St. Upper
Stephen St. Lower
Grafton St.
Dawson St.
Kildare St.
National Museums
St. Patrick's Park
Whitefriar St.
Mercer St. Lower
King St. South
Gaiety Theatre
Mansion House
The Shelbourne Hotel
St. Patrick's Cathedral
Aungier St.
Peter Row
York St.
St. Stephen's Green West
St. Stephen's Green North
Merrion Row
Kevin St. Upper
St. Stephen's Green Park

What is it about this country that has produced so many great authors, poets, and artists? And what is it about Dublin that draws them to move here and use the city for their inspiration to write books about the Irish experience that move us all? Here is your chance to ponder these mysteries as you pound the pavement in the footsteps of James Joyce, George Bernard Shaw, Jonathan Swift, and Brendan Behan, among others. This walk takes you to some of their homes, their favorite pubs, their churches, and their libraries. See if it inspires you. START: **Bus 11, 13 & 16 to Eccles St.**

❶ ★★ The Hugh Lane Gallery.

One of the best art galleries in Dublin, the fairly small permanent collection includes some real big hitters from the Impressionist canon—including works by Degas and Rodin. There are also plenty of works from contemporary Irish artists. An unusual highlight of the collection is the studio of the Irish painter Francis Bacon (1909–1992). Bacon, who was one of the true giants of 20th-century figurative art, spent most of his life in London—from where his studio was removed (clutter and all) and painstakingly pieced back together at the gallery, where it's been on display since 2001. ⏱ *1 hr. Parnell Sq. North. See p 13,* ❷.

❷ ★★ Dublin Writers Museum.

Manuscripts, early editions, personal possessions, and other pieces of ephemera relating to Ireland's most famous writers are on display at this great museum in Parnell Square. The exhibits are laid out across two rooms, tracing the development of Irish literature up to the present day. Lovers of Behan, Joyce, Shaw, Stoker, Wilde, Yeats, and the other greats of the canon will find plenty to love here—from the trivial (Brendan Behan's postcard from Los Angeles extolling its virtues as a place to get drunk) to the profound (a first edition of Patrick Kavanagh's *The Great Hunger,* complete with a handwritten extra section that his publisher refused to publish, fearing it too controversial). You can take a self-guided audio tour, and there's an excellent bookshop—of course. Talks, readings, and other special events are occasionally held here; call or check the website for details. ⏱ *1 hr. 18 Parnell Sq. See p 13,* ❶.

The Hugh Lane Gallery, Charlemont House.

❸ ★ James Joyce Centre. This idiosyncratic museum is set in a handsome Georgian house that once belonged to the Earl of Kenmare. Joyce himself never lived here; he was, however, rather taken with a former owner of the house named Denis Maginni—an eccentric Irishman who added an "i" to his name to give himself an air of Italian sophistication. (Maginni appears as a character in Joyce's masterpiece *Ulysses*.) Today the center functions as both a small museum and a cultural center devoted to Joyce and his work. Actual exhibits are a little thin on the ground, but they hold interesting (at least for Joyce fans) lectures and special events, and also organize a Joyce-themed walking tour of Dublin. Unsurprisingly, this place becomes an explosion of activity around Bloomsday (June 16th), the date upon which *Ulysses'* fictional events take place. Unlike the rest of Dublin, which makes do with a single day of celebrating its most famous 20th-century literary hero, the James Joyce Centre turns it into a week-long festival. ⏱ *45 min. 35 North Great George's St. www.jamesjoyce.ie.* ☎ *01/878-8547. Admission €5 adults; €4 seniors, students & children. Apr–Sept Mon–Sat 10am–5pm, Sun noon–5pm; Oct–Mar Tues–Sat noon–5pm, Sun noon–5pm. Last admission 30 min. before closing. Bus: 1, 4, 7.*

❹ ★ James Joyce statue. You've probably seen the book (real or electronic), viewed his study, and seen his hero's door—now you can see what JJ looked like. This life-size sculpture portrays Joyce's characteristic nonchalant stance as he leans on his cane, thereby provoking the locals' unflattering nickname the "Prick with the Stick." ⏱ *5 min. Corner O'Connell St. & N. Earl St.*

❺ ★★ Marsh's Library. Unlike Trinity College's Long Room, which is largely for show these days, Marsh's Library is still a functioning library. Founded by Narcissus Marsh, the Archbishop of Dublin, in 1701, its interior is a magnificent example of a 17th-century scholar's library and has remained much the same for 3 centuries. Its walls are lined with scholarly volumes, chiefly focused on theology, medicine, ancient history, and maps, along with Hebrew, Greek, Latin, and French literature. You can still see the wire cages in which readers would be locked in with the more valuable tomes. There's a particularly excellent collection of books by and about Jonathan Swift, which includes volumes with his editing comments in the margins—ironically, perhaps, given that Swift himself said of Archbishop Marsh, "He is the first of human race, that with great advantages of learning, piety, and station ever escaped being a great man." ⏱ *45 min. St Patrick's Close. www.marshlibrary.ie.* ☎ *01/454-3511. Admission €3 adults; €2 seniors & students; children under 16 free. Mon, Wed–Fri 9:30am–5pm; Sat 10am–5pm. Closed public holidays & last week in Dec. Bus: inc. 49, 150, 151.*

James Joyce statue.

National Library of Ireland.

⑥ ★ National Library of Ireland. If you're coming to Ireland to research your roots, this library should be one of your first stops, with thousands of volumes and records that yield ancestral information. Open at this location since 1890, this is also the principal library of Irish studies, particularly noted for its collection of first editions and the papers of Irish writers and political figures, such as W. B. Yeats, Daniel O'Connell, and Patrick Pearse. Parts of the collection are always on display to the general public (the exhibition devoted to Yeats is particularly good). The library also has an unrivaled collection of maps of Ireland. A specialist **Genealogy Advisory Service** is open Monday to Friday from 9:30am to 4:45pm. It's free of charge; no appointment necessary. ⏱ *45 min. Kildare St. www.nli.ie.* ☎ *01/603-0200. Free admission. Mon–Wed 9:30am–7:45pm; Thurs–Sat 9:30am–4:45pm (reading rooms close 12:45pm on Sat), Sun 1–4:45pm (exhibits only, reading rooms closed). DART: Pearse. Bus: inc. 7B, 10, 15.*

⑦ ★★ Temple Bar Gallery. Quintessentially Temple Bar, this large art gallery is packed with interesting, often groundbreaking, work by contemporary Irish visual artists. You can also book an appointment to watch some of the artists at work in the studios here. Part of the appeal of this gallery is its wonderful eclecticism, with a variety of disciplines represented: painting, sculpture, photography, printmaking, and more. The gallery also hosts regular talks and other public events. Best of all, it's free! ⏱ *1½ hr. 5–9 Temple Bar. www. templebargallery.com.* ☎ *01/671-0073. Free admission. Tues–Sat 11am–6pm. Bus: 26, 37, 39.*

⑧ ★★★ Literary Pub Crawl. Hopefully you've had a chance to rest a little before the last stop on today's tour, because your hard-working feet have a final challenge ahead—albeit one that hardly seems like work. Of the several good walking tours of Dublin available, this is one of our favorites. Walking in the footsteps of Joyce, Behan, Beckett, Shaw, and other Irish literary greats, the tour visits Dublin's most famous pubs and explores their deep literary connections. Actors provide humorous performances and commentary between stops. Tours, which involve about a half mile of walking, start from the **Duke Pub**, on Duke Street, daily at 7:30pm April to October and Thursday to Sunday at 7:30pm November to March. A limited number of tickets are sold at the Duke on the night, but it's best to book online. No children are allowed. ⏱ *2¼ hr. Starts 7:30pm at the Duke Pub, Duke St. www.dublin-pubcrawl.com.* ☎ *01/670-5602. Tickets €12 adults, €10 students. DART: Pearse. Bus: inc. 10, 11A, 13.*

Dublin with Kids

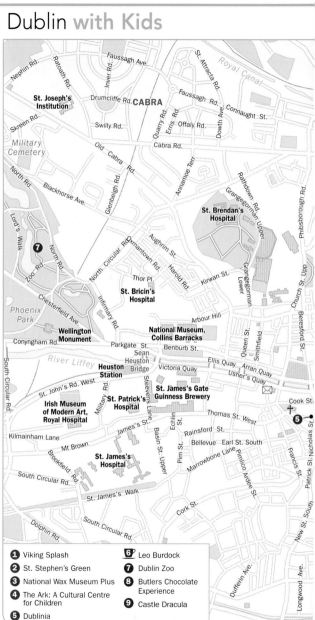

① Viking Splash
② St. Stephen's Green
③ National Wax Museum Plus
④ The Ark: A Cultural Centre for Children
⑤ Dublinia
⑥ Leo Burdock
⑦ Dublin Zoo
⑧ Butlers Chocolate Experience
⑨ Castle Dracula

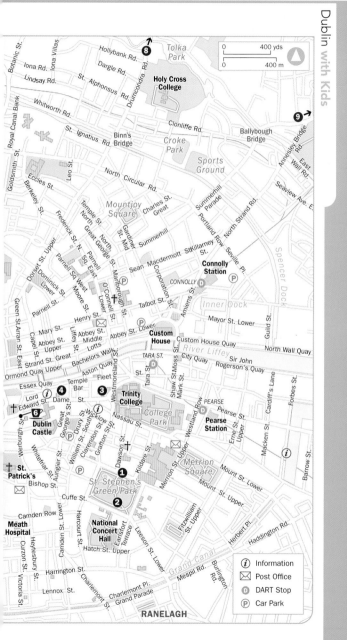

From themed museums to vast parks, there's entertainment galore to keep the kids amused. Don't attempt to do all these in a day; just select venues suitable for your children's age and interests. To relax, Dublin's outdoor spaces are brilliant, and remember that the national museums and galleries all have activity packs for the little ones. (See also chapter 5.) START: **All cross city buses to St. Stephen's Green.**

❶ ★ Viking Splash Tour. This entertaining tour by land and sea led by a costumed guide gives an amusing take on the city, touching on its Viking history and also pointing out historic highlights. Traveling on a "Duck"—a 7-ton amphibious World War II tank—kids (and adults if they wish) get to wear Viking helmets and roar at passers-by. Endure the inevitable squeals as the tank then launches into the water for a tour around the Docklands. Tours depart roughly every half hour from 10am in summer, less often in winter; call to prebook, and check daily schedule. ⏱ *1 hr., 15 min. Pickup point St. Stephen's Green N. Reservations recommended:* ☎ *01/707-6000. www.vikingsplash.ie. Admission €22 adults, €20 seniors & students, €17 children 13–17, €12 children 2–12. Daily every 30 min from 10am–5pm. Bus: All buses to St. Stephen's Green.*

Viking Splash Tour.

❷ ★ St. Stephen's Green. This bucolic expanse is a must for young kids to run around—and all enjoy feeding the ducks: Walk to the pond, to the left of the Fusiliers' Arch entrance, and dispense with your leftover sandwiches. There's also a children's playground near the center of the green. It's easy to visualize when this was once prime pram-pushing territory back in Georgian times, such are the lovely willows, flowerbeds, and the general benefits of a green oasis in the city. During summer, there are occasional free plays performed in the amphitheater, and lunchtime music recitals in the bandstand. ⏱ *45 min. Luas: St. Stephen's Green. Bus: inc. 20B, 32X, 33X.*

❸ ★ National Wax Museum Plus. Ireland's answer to Madame Tussaud's, this small museum occupies the former armory of the Parliament House (see p 9). It's mostly aimed at kids, with more hands-on, interactive attractions beyond the usual wax tableaux (hence the "Plus"). At the "Wax Factor" studio, you can sing along to a variety of pop hits and have yourself superimposed into the videos while you do it (take away a DVD for €7), and in the Wax Hands room you can have a wax model of your hand made, because who wouldn't want that? The waxwork galleries themselves include displays on Irish history and mythology; great Irish writers; and, perhaps most successfully, the Chamber of Horrors, which sometimes features live actors waiting to

Feeding ducks in St. Stephen's Green.

administer additional scares (16 and older only). ⏱ *1 hr. 4 Foster Pl. www.waxmuseumplus.ie.* ☎ *01/645-8813. Admission €12 adults; €10 seniors, students & children 13—17; €8 children 5—12 (children 4 & under free); €35 families. Daily 10—7; last admission 45 min before closing. Bus: inc. 9, 13, 16.*

④ ★ The Ark: a Cultural Centre for Children. This is a great option for children who are makers, thinkers, doers, listeners, and watchers. Age-specific programs are geared to small groups of kids from 2 to 12 years old. Mini-courses (1–2 hr. long) are designed around themes in music, visual arts, and theater; there are also workshops in photography, instrument making, and the art of architecture. The custom-designed arts center has three modern floors that house a theater, a gallery, and a workshop for hands-on learning sessions. Tickets include one child and one adult; prices vary, but expect to pay around €6 to €12 for most events. Check the current themes and schedule on the Ark's very helpful website and book well ahead. ⏱ *2 hr. 11A Eustace St. www.ark.ie.* ☎ *01/670-7788. Ticket prices vary. Event times vary; call ahead. DART: Tara St. Luas: Jervis. Bus: inc. 27, 40, 49.*

⑤ ★ Dublinia. Covering the history of Dublin from the Viking age through medieval times, this child-friendly history "experience" is presented as a series of interactive tableaux—complete with sound effects, smells, and audio "reconstructions" of *olde worlde* Dublin. (They're such effective earworms, in fact, that even adults may find themselves thinking about them months later.) Kids can try on clothes like the ones their ancestors may have worn, or even find themselves placed in the Dublin stocks as "felons." Check the website for details of special tours, with costumed guides, and other family-friendly activities. Dublinia is right across from Christ Church Cathedral, making this an excellent payoff for any little ones who patiently trudged around that historic but austere building; combined tickets for the two offer big savings. ⏱ *1 hr. St. Michael's Hill. www.dublinia.ie.* ☎ *01/679-4611. Admission €8.50 adults; €7.50 seniors & students; €5.50 children; €24 families. Mar–Sept daily 10am–6:30pm; Oct–Feb daily 10am–5:30pm. Last admission 1 hr. before closing. Luas: Four Courts. Bus: 49, 49A, 54A, 123.*

Wax Museum.

6 ★ Leo Burdock's. Ireland's most famous fish & chips shop now has several branches, but this is the original. Join the great and the good who have come before you to sample the tasty traditional treat. *2 Wenburgh St.* ☎ *01/454-0306. $.*

7 ★★ Dublin Zoo. If you've got kids and they're in need of a change from castles, churches, and history, here's the antidote. This modern, humane zoo in Phoenix Park provides a home for more than 235 species of wild animals and tropical birds. The animals live

Dublinia medieval boat.

inside a series of realistically created habitats such as "African Savanna," home to giraffes, rhinos, and ostriches; "Gorilla Rainforest," a 12,000-square-meter (7½ sq.-mile) enclosure that houses five lowland gorillas; "Asian Forest," home to Sumatran tigers and lions; "the South American House," with an eclectic range of almost unbearably cute species, including tiny pygmy marmosets and two-toed sloths; and the "Pacific Coast," opened in 2015, home to sea lions (you can watch them swim underwater) and a flamingo aviary big enough for the gracious birds to take flight. Playgrounds and gift shops are scattered throughout. Feeding times and scheduled talks are posted on the zoo's website (several times daily Mar–Sept; weekends only Oct–Feb). A restaurant is on site, as well as plenty of smaller cafes and picnic areas for those who prefer to bring their own meals. ⏲ *2 hr. Phoenix Park. www.dublinzoo.ie.* ☎ *01/474-8900. Admission €17.50 adults; €13.50 seniors & students; €12.50 children 3–15; €5.80 special needs child; €9.20 special needs adult; €48–€58 families. Mar–Sept daily 9:30am–6pm; Oct 9:30am–5:30pm; Nov–Dec 9:30am–4pm; Jan 9:30am–4:30pm;*

Feb 9:30am–5pm. Last admission to zoo 1 hr. before closing; last admission to African Savanna 30 min. before closing. Luas: Heuston (15-min. walk). Bus: inc. 25, 26, 66.

8 ★★ Butlers Chocolate Experience.

Ireland is awash with brewery tours, but rare is the chance to look around a real-life chocolate factory. The world-famous chocolatiers, whose cafes are scattered throughout Dublin, have been based in the city since the 1930s. The delectable confections are now produced at a less-than-lovely industrial park on the road to Malahide, but like all the best soft-centered chocolates, the sweet part is on the inside. The tour takes you around the factory to see the luxury chocolate makers in action. (Don't worry, there are plenty of tastings.) The factory is completely accessible to wheelchair users. You have to book tours in advance and space is quite limited. No chocolates are made on Saturday, so the weekday tours are definitely the most fun. ⏱ 2 hr. *Clonshagh Business & Technology Park, Oscar Traynor Rd. (From Dublin take R105 to R107 toward Malahide; after about 3.5km [2½ miles], turn left onto Oscar Traynor Rd., take fifth right turn and look for sign on the left.) www.butlerschocolates.com/chocolateexperience.* ☎ 01/851-2151. Admission €13 adults; €48 families. Mon–Sat 10am, noon & 3:30pm. Booking essential. Bus: 130.

9 ★ Castle Dracula.

One for older kids only (under 14s are not allowed), this part-museum, part-live show is certainly a novel way to spend a Saturday night. It's all presented as an homage to Dublin-born author Bram Stoker, as your tour of "Castle Dracula" takes you through a series of elaborately constructed sets and tunnels.

Costumed actors try to scare you and make you laugh in almost equal measure, while you learn more about Bram Stoker and the Dracula phenomenon along the way. (They even have a real lock of Stoker's hair, allegedly taken from his corpse by his wife.) The tour ends in an underground auditorium made to look like a spooky graveyard, where you watch a live show that includes comedy and two magicians. The emphasis overall is on laughs rather than scares (the fact that they also claim not to allow pregnant women on the tour is a fairly ridiculous gimmick). You meet at the reception lobby of the Westwood Club, a modern gym, which somehow adds to the bizarreness of the whole experience. Tickets must be booked in advance. Clontarf DART station is literally next door, or it's about a 15-minute cab ride from the center of Dublin. ⏱ 2 hr. Meet at West-wood Gym, Clontarf Rd. www.castle dracula.ie. ☎ 01/851-2151. Admission €25 adults; €20 seniors, students & children 15–18. Late Feb–Aug Sat only 7pm (arrive 6:45pm). May not run every week—check website for schedule. DART: Clontarf. Bus: 130.

Butlers Chocolate Experience.

Trinity College

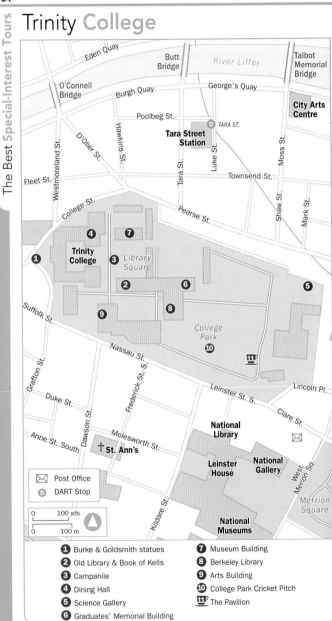

1 Burke & Goldsmith statues
2 Old Library & Book of Kells
3 Campanile
4 Dining Hall
5 Science Gallery
6 Graduates' Memorial Building
7 Museum Building
8 Berkeley Library
9 Arts Building
10 College Park Cricket Pitch
11 The Pavilion

ating back to 1592, Ireland's oldest college has seen great writers and esteemed academics graduate from its hallowed halls—not all of them complimentary: Samuel Beckett allegedly quipped "Trinity's graduates were like cream: thick and rich." Established by Queen Elizabeth I, Trinity forbid Catholics to join unless they accepted the Protestant faith, restrictions only lifted in 1970. START: **Bus 15, 50, & 77 to College St.**

1 Burke & Goldsmith statues.

Guarding the Regent House entrance to Trinity are the imposing statues of Edmund Burke and Oliver Goldsmith, cast in white marble by 19th-century sculptor John Henry Foley. Burke (1729–97) became a British statesman thanks to his prowess in political philosophy. Author of *She Stoops to Conquer*, Goldsmith (1728–74) had a colorful life after graduating in theology and law from Trinity; he studied medicine in Edinburgh and traveled through Europe before becoming a noted poet and playwright.

2 Old Library & Book of

Kells. Inside the grand Old Library, a huge, majestic paneled hall containing more than 200,000 books, visitors line up around the block for this one. The illuminated copy of the Book of Kells, four gospels written in Latin around A.D. 800, is lavishly decorated and one of the most famous books in the world. Two volumes are displayed in glass cases, and, as part of the complete **Turning Darkness into Light** exhibition, the Book of Armagh and the even older Book of Durrow are also on display. If, however, you dislike peering through crowds for a glimpse, try around 1pm when the hordes may have thinned out a little. Even if it's hard to get a proper look at the Book, the view down the length of the Old Library is outstanding. ⏱ *1 hr. See p 9,* 6.

The Campanile, Trinity College.

3 Campanile. The most striking

and famous monument inside Trinity's grounds, the white Campanile, or belltower, grabs your attention as you enter through the main archway. Dating back to the mid-19th century, built by Sir Charles Lanyon, it stands on the site of the college's original foundations from 400 years earlier. Walk all the way around and gaze up at its peak—it looks even better in the sunshine.

4 Dining Hall. Here's a real treat:

The immensely high-ceilinged hall and wooden paneling make even your cup of tea and scone seem special. The building was originally designed by Richard Castle in the 1740s, but after collapsing twice, was rebuilt by Hugh Darley around 1760. Damaged yet again, this time by fire in 1984, it underwent a

Trinity College: Practical Matters

Covering a vast 16 hectares (40 acres), this oasis of cobbled, sculpture-filled green lies calmly in the city center. Be prepared for long lines outside the Old Library to see the Book of Kells, with occasional temporary closure for visiting foreign dignitaries. In summer, it's worth buying a combined ticket that includes entrance to the Book of Kells, plus a guided walk of the college campus led by a student for just an extra couple of euros. Admission to the Book of Kells and Old Library: €10 adults, €9 seniors, students and children, €20 families; with a campus tour, it's €13 adults, €12 seniors and students, and €26 families. Opening times for the Book of Kells and Old Library: June–Sept Mon–Sat 9am–6pm, Sun 9:30am–6pm; Oct–May Mon–Sat 9:30am–5pm, Sun noon–4:30pm. Tours: May–Sept daily 10:15am–3:40pm, about every 40 min. www. tcd.ie. ☎ 01/896-1000.

prize-winning restoration. Visitors can pop in for an inexpensive lunch and gaze at the portrait-filled walls.

5 ★ Science Gallery. This museum takes a science-is-fun approach, with interactive, high-tech exhibitions. It's not as lightweight as it sounds, however, and the displays are genuinely interesting—you really can learn something about the latest developments in a variety of fields. ⏱ *45 min. www. sciencegallery.com.* ☎ *01-896 4091. Free admission. Tues–Fri noon–8pm; Sat–Sun noon–6pm.*

6 Graduates' Memorial Building. The GMB now houses student accommodation—streets ahead of the sort I had to endure—and is also home to the university's history and philosophical societies. The neo-Gothic Victorian building was designed by Sir Thomas Drew in 1892, one of 19th-century Ireland's most distinguished architects. It's not possible to enter, but walk around the outside for a closer look at some of the detailed stonework.

7 Museum Building. Home to the geography and geology departments, this is one of my favorite Dublin hidden gems. Designed by architects Dean and Woodward, with stonemasonry by the famed O'Shea brothers, this

Trinity College Museum Building.

mid-19th-century creation has intriguing Byzantine and Moorish influences. Samuel Haughton, inventor of the "humane hangman's drop" was a professor here in the late 19th century. Enter through the main door past two enormous skeletons of giant Irish deer, and check out the domed ceiling and green marbled banisters. Visit the small but absorbing **Geology Museum** on the top floor. *Geology Museum:* ☎ *01-896 1477. Free admission. Mon–Fri 10am–5pm.*

⑧ Berkley Library Building. Directly next door, this mid-20th-century addition to the campus sharply divides opinion with its austere modernism. Designer Paul Koralek's library honors Bishop George Berkeley, famed for his philosophical theory of "immaterialism" (things that can't be proved cannot exist), which went against the theories of both Isaac Newton and the Catholic Church. The gleaming sculpture outside the library is *Sphere with Sphere* by Arnaldo Pomodoro (1983).

⑨ Arts Building. Also facing the Old Library across Fellows Square, the 1970s Arts Building includes the **Douglas Hyde Gallery,** which displays a regularly changing program of modern art. Exhibitions switch out about every 3 months and admission is always free.

⑩ College Park Cricket Pitch. One of the more benign remnants of English rule, this is a small park where you'll often find a cricket match in progress on summer weekends. If you don't know the rules of cricket, it may be hard to follow—the sport is notoriously arcane for the uninitiated—but you can still enjoy the picturesque sight of the players in their white uniforms.

⑪ ★ The Pavilion. Located on the eastern side of the College Park Cricket Pitch, this popular bar and cafe has a balcony from which you can watch play. ☎ *01-896 1279. $.*

Vikings & Medieval Dubh Linn

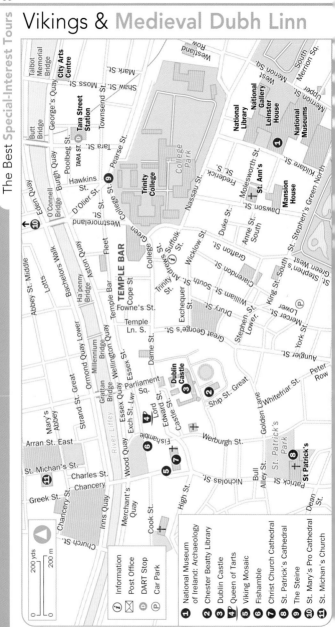

- *i* Information
- ✉ Post Office
- Ⓓ DART Stop
- Ⓟ Car Park

- ❶ National Museum of Ireland: Archaeology
- ❷ Chester Beatty Library
- ❸ Dublin Castle
- ❹ Queen of Tarts
- ❺ Viking Mosaic
- ❻ Fishamble
- ❼ Christ Church Cathedral
- ❽ St. Patrick's Cathedral
- ❾ The Steine
- ❿ St. Mary's Pro Cathedral
- ⓫ St. Michan's Church

Visitors come to see Dublin's literary and political history, yet its Viking past is lesser known. When two fleets of Norsemen arrived on the Liffey in A.D. 837 and established camp near today's Dublin Castle, they named it *An Dubh Linn* (literally "Black Pool"). This tour shows off some of the fascinating remains of that era, especially around Temple Bar, Wood Quay, and Dublin Castle. START: **Bus 7, 10, 11, & 13 to Merrion Row.**

① ★★★ National Museum of Ireland: Archaeology. The most impressive of the four sites that collectively make up the National Museum of Ireland, this excellent museum is devoted to the ancient history of Ireland and beyond—from the Stone Age up to the Early Modern period. Highlights include a stunning collection of Viking artifacts from the archaeological digs that took place in Dublin from the 1960s to the early 1980s—a haul so important that in one fell swoop the history of Viking settlement in Ireland was rewritten. There is also an enormous range of Bronze Age gold and metalwork, as well as iconic Christian treasures from the Dark Ages, including the **Ardagh Chalice,** the **Moylough Belt Shrine,** and the **Tara Brooch.** Other notable artifacts **include "Ralaghan Man,"** a carved wooden Bronze Age statue from County Cavan; a collection of 2nd-century Roman figurines and homewares; and an extraordinary granite table made in Egypt circa 1870 B.C. ⏱ *2 hr. Kildare St. See p 10, ⑨.*

② ★★★ Chester Beatty Library. From one great museum to another, and this really is a hidden gem. Located on the grounds of Dublin Castle, the Chester Beatty isn't particularly big—it holds just two permanent galleries, plus space for temporary exhibitions—and yet this is always at the top of our list when people ask for recommendations of where to visit in Dublin. The collection of early religious texts and other priceless works of art is named in honor of Sir Alfred Chester Beatty, an Anglo-American industrialist who bequeathed his unique private collection to the Irish nation when he died in 1968. And what a collection it was! Beatty was one of the great 20th-century adventurer-collectors, of the kind that simply could not exist today. Highlights of the bequest include breathtaking illuminated gospels and early Bibles (including the oldest known fragment in existence, from 150 A.D.); beautiful 15th-century Quarans that look as if they were finished yesterday; scrolls from the 8th and 9th centuries; and sacred early Buddhist texts from Burma. Recent acquisitions include an epic and colorful 17th-century Japanese scroll running nearly twice the length of a gallery; and a collection of extremely steamy Egyptian love letters dating from 1800 B.C. (On a recent visit the security guard told us they couldn't display the

The National Museum of Ireland: Archaeology.

translations as they were so explicit they would "make my priest's rosary beads melt".) ⏱ *1 hr. Dame St. See p 7,* **❷**.

❸ ★ Dublin Castle. For nearly 8 centuries this was the focus for British rule in Ireland, from its construction in the 1200s to when it was finally taken over by the new Irish government in 1922. You can wander the grounds for free, but they're somewhat plain; the official tour takes in the much more impressive State Apartments, the early 18th-century Treasury, and the Chapel Royal chapel, built in the Gothic style, with fine plaster decoration and a carved-oak gallery. The castle's only extant tower—a 13th-century structure once used to imprison suspected traitors—now holds a small museum dedicated to the Garda (Irish police). The castle's Upper Yard was, in 1583, the scene of Ireland's last trial by mortal combat; today it is dominated by an impressive Georgian structure called the **Bedford Tower.** The Irish crown jewels used to be kept in the Bedford Tower—until they were stolen in 1907 (and have never been found). If it's open, check out the **Medieval Undercroft,** an excavated site on the grounds where an early Viking fortress once stood.

Chester Beatty Library.

Note: This is a government building, so some areas may be closed for state events. ⏱ *1 hr. Dame St. See p 7,* **❶**.

❹ ★ Queen of Tarts. This cheerful little tearoom in the heart of Temple Bar is a delightful pit stop for a pot of tea and some form of sweet, diet-busting snack. *Cork Hill.* ☎ *01-633 4681. $.*

❺ ★ Viking Mosaic. Adjacent to Christ Church Cathedral, at the southern end of Winetavern Street, look down at the pavement. In dark stone, you'll see the full-sized plan of a typical early Viking building site. While you're in the vicinity, look out for bronze slabs in the pavement, including one outside the main entrance to Christ Church Cathedral, indicating the locations of artifacts excavated. You can see the real things in the National Museum (see above). *Winetavern St.*

❻ ★ Fishamble. Now filled with pubs and clubs, this was the hub of medieval Dublin, and a few relics remain. Fishamble, the oldest street, was the original location of the fish market. Look or the plaque on the wall next to the **George Frederic Handel Hotel** (no. 16–18),

Courtyard of Dublin Castle.

marking the spot of the former "Musick Hall"; this was the venue of the world's first performance of Handel's *Messiah*—which he also conducted—on April 13, 1742. Look for the Turk's Head bar on Essex Gate—outside that and the Czech Inn (formerly Isolde's Tower) opposite are two stone pillars marking the original city gates.

⓻ ★★ Christ Church Cathedral. This magnificent cathedral, just around the corner from Dublin Castle, was designed to impress visitors who approached from the River Liffey. It dates from 1038, when Sitric, Danish king of Dublin, built the first wooden Christ Church here. In 1171, the original foundation was extended into a cruciform layout by the Anglo-Norman warrior, Strongbow (who led the first English invasion of Ireland). The present structure dates mainly from 1871 to 1878, when a huge restoration took place—the work done then remains controversial to this day, as much of the building's old detail was destroyed in the process. Still, magnificent stonework and graceful pointed arches survive. (There's also a statue of Strongbow inside, and some believe his tomb is here as well, although historians

are not convinced.) The best way to get a glimpse of what the original building must have been like is to visit the 12th-century crypt, which has been kept untouched. Right opposite the Christ Church, Dublinia (see p 31) does a lively job of telling the story of Viking and medieval Dublin, although it's mostly for kids. ⓘ 45 min. Christchurch Pl. See p 8, ❸.

⓼ ★★ St. Patrick's Cathedral. The largest church in Ireland, and one of the most beloved places of worship in the world, St. Patrick's is

St. Patrick's Day in front of Christ Church Cathedral.

the other of the great Anglican cathedrals in Dublin. Most of the visible building is from the 14th century, but religious buildings were on the site for almost a thousand years before that. The cathedral mostly follows the traditional style of early English church buildings, including a square medieval tower that contains the largest set of ringing peal bells in Ireland. The spire is 18th century. A moving collection of war memorials is tucked away at the very back of the cavernous nave, including a very low-key tribute to the Irish dead of World War II. (Ireland was neutral in that war, but around 300,000 men volunteered to fight with the Allies.) Admission includes an irregular program of lunchtime classical music recitals at the cathedral—call or check the website for details. *Tip:* You can download an MP3 audio tour from the Cathedral's website for €2.50; click "Visit Us" then "Audio Guide." ○ *45 min. St. Patrick's Close. See p 8,* ❹.

❾ ★ **The Steine.** Traffic whizzes around one of Dublin's busiest roundabouts, yet its center marks where the Vikings first landed. The Steine, a granite slab, represents the original Standing Stones,

360–420cm (12–14 ft) high, that the Vikings erected in the 10th or 11th centuries to mark the boundaries of their Dublin territories. This one is a reproduction, carved by Cliodna Cussen, depicting the faces of Ivor, the 9th-century Viking King of Dublin. In front is the **Townsend Street police station,** once the headquarters of the Garda and where Michael Collins entered secretly during the 1916 uprising to take a peek at the records. *Junction of D'Olier, Townsend & College sts.*

❿ ★ **St. Mary's Pro Cathedral.** No, there isn't a pro and amateur league for cathedrals in Ireland—"pro" simply means "temporary." And therein lies a fascinating piece of historical trivia. Contrary to popular belief, Dublin has no Roman Catholic Cathedral (St. Patrick's and Christ Church have been part of the Anglican Church of Ireland since the 16th century.) But the Vatican views Christ Church as Dublin's "true" Catholic Cathedral. Therefore, St. Mary's has been designated the "temporary" official Catholic cathedral in Dublin . . . since 1820. Tucked away on a rather unimpressive back street, it's nonetheless the heart of the city's Northside. It was built between 1815 and

The Steine, the center of Dublin where the Vikings first landed.

1825 in Greek Revival Doric style, with an exterior portico modeled on the Temple of Theseus in Athens, with six Doric columns. The Renaissance-style interior is patterned after the Church of Saint-Philippe du Roule of Paris. The church is noted for its awe-inspiring Palestrina Choir, which sings a Latin Mass every Sunday at 11am (during school term times). ⏱ *30 min. 83 Marlborough St. www.pro cathedral.ie.* ☎ *01/874-5441. Free admission. Mon–Fri 7:30am–6:30pm; Sat 7:30am–7pm; Sun 9am–2pm, 5:30–7:30pm; public holidays 10am–1:30pm. DART: Connolly, Tara St. Luas: Abbey St. Bus: 2, 3, 4.*

⓫ ★★ St. Michan's Church.
Built on the site of an early Danish chapel (1095), this 17th-century edifice has fine interior woodwork and an organ (dated 1724) on which Handel is said to have played his *Messiah*. But the church is more famous for its two underground crypts—one of which is filled with mummified bodies that have lain for centuries in an extraordinary state of preservation. A few still have their hair and fingernails; on others you can see desiccated internal organs under the skin. The tallest mummy is known as "the Crusader"; his legs were broken in order to fit him into the coffin. Others in residence include "the Nun" and "the Thief"; their true identities were lost when the church records were destroyed during the civil war in 1922. It's a macabre place, but fascinating. Word is that Bram Stoker was inspired to write *Dracula* in part by having visited as a child. **Note:** The church is wheelchair accessible, but the vaults are not. ⏱ *45 min. Church St., Dublin 7. See p 20,* ❻ *.*

Revolutionary Dublin

1 Kilmainham Gaol
2 Áras an Uachtaráin
3 The Four Courts
4 Garden of Remembrance
5 Charles Stuart Parnell
6 General Post Office
7 Jim Larkin statue
8 Daniel O'Connell statue
9 Glasnevin Cemetery & Museum

i Information
⊠ Post Office
Ⓓ DART Stop
Ⓟ Car Park

The history of Ireland is dominated by revolution. Waves of invaders have tried to claim the country for themselves, from the Vikings in the first millennium to the English in the second. Of course, the English took rather longer to get rid of—after several failed revolutions, Ireland finally became an independent nation in 1922. Dublin is filled with places where you can learn about that long and difficult struggle—and some that still bear scars. START: **All cross-city buses to St. Stephen's Green.**

❶ ★★★ Kilmainham Gaol. Anyone interested in Ireland's struggle for independence from British rule should not miss visiting this former prison. Within these walls, political prisoners were incarcerated, tortured, and killed, from 1796 until 1924. The leaders of the 1916 Easter Uprising were executed here, along with many others. Future president Eamon de Valera was its final prisoner. An exhibition illuminates the brutal history of the Irish penal system; there's also a well-presented historical film. To walk along these corridors through the grim exercise yard, or to venture into the walled compound, is a moving (at times even overwhelming) experience that will linger in your memory. 🕐 *2 hr. Inchicore Rd. See p 19, ❶.*

❷ ★★ Áras an Uachtaráin. Set in Phoenix Park, Áras an Uachtaráin was once the Viceregal Lodge, the summer retreat of the British viceroy, whose main digs were in Dublin Castle. The original 1751 country house was expanded several times, gradually becoming the splendid neoclassical white mansion you see today. Although Ireland finally won independence from Britain in 1922, its constitutional position was somewhat hazy for a while afterwards—the British monarch remained ceremonial head of state until 1937, and it wasn't a full Republic until 1948. The Lodge was renamed Áras an Uachtaráin ("President's House") in 1938, and has been the official residence of the President ever since. Guided tours leave from the Phoenix Park Visitors Centre every Saturday. After an introductory historical film, a bus brings visitors to and from the house for a 1-hour tour of the state reception rooms (tours run a little

Áras an Uachtarain, Phoenix Park residence of the Irish President.

longer in summer, when the gardens are included on the itinerary, weather permitting). Because the building is still the official home of the Irish president, a strictly limited number of tickets are given out, on a first-come, first-served basis. The house may occasionally be closed for state events, so it's wise to call ahead. *Note:* For security reasons, no backpacks, travel bags, strollers, cameras, or mobile phones are allowed on the tour. ⏱ *1½ hr. Tour departs from Phoenix Park Visitor Centre. www.president.ie. ☎ 01/677-0095 (Phoenix Park visitor center). Free admission. Sat tours hourly, 10:30am–3:30pm. Bus: 37.*

❸ ★ The Four Courts. Built between 1786 and 1802, this imposing building has been home to the highest courts in Ireland ever since. (Although it should presumably be called the "Three Courts" nowadays, since one of them, the Central Criminal Court, moved out in 2010.) The building saw some of the worst fighting in the Easter Rising of 1916, when it housed the 1st Battalion of the rebel army. It saw even more intense fighting during the Civil War of 1922, when the building was all but devastated. It was painstakingly restored over the subsequent decade, although some details, such as the statues of famous Irish lawyers that once adorned the niches of the Round Hall, were beyond repair. But the most tragic loss, it is now believed, was an accident—over a thousand years' worth of public records went up in flames when an Irish Republican Army (IRA) ammunition store was mistakenly detonated. Tours of the Four Courts are available, but frustratingly only for law students (who must book as part of a group). Otherwise, to see the interior you can go watch a trial in progress. ⏱ *15 min. Inns Quay. See p 21, ❼.*

❹ ★ Garden of Remembrance. Before hitting busy O'Connell Street, take time out to relax in this tranquil garden, opened in 1966 to commemorate the 50th anniversary of the Easter Rising and all those who died during the struggle for Irish freedom. It's dominated by the cross-shaped water feature, leading the eye to Oisin Kelly's immense cast-iron sculpture, which is based on the theme of the Children of Lir, its birds in flight symbolizing rebirth and resurrection. ⏱ *15 min. East Parnell Square.*

❺ ★ Charles Stuart Parnell statue. The bronze statue of Parnell, born to a wealthy Protestant landowner in 1846, dominates the northern end of O'Connell Street. After being elected to Parliament in 1878, he opposed the Irish land laws and became the accepted leader of the Irish nationalist movement. Advocating a boycott to influence landlords, he was sent to Kilmainham. After his release he joined the Liberal party, which successfully introduced the first Irish Home Rule Bill. Sadly Parnell's reputation was ruined when his

Charles Stuart Parnell statue.

long-standing affair with Kitty O'Shea (with whom he had three children) surfaced when her husband filed for divorce. ○ *5 min. Corner of Upper O'Connell St. & Parnell St.*

❻ ★ General Post Office (GPO). Don't be fooled by the nondescript name: With a facade of Ionic columns and Greco-Roman pilasters 60m long (197 ft.) and 17m high (56 ft.), this is more than a post office—it is the symbol of Irish freedom. Built between 1815 and 1818, it was the main stronghold of the Irish Volunteers during the Easter Rising. On Easter Sunday, 1916, Patrick Pearse stood on its steps and read a proclamation declaring a free Irish Republic. It began, "In every generation the Irish people have asserted their right to national freedom and sovereignty." Then he and an army of supporters barricaded themselves inside. A siege ensued that ultimately involved much of the north of the city, and before it was over, the building was all but destroyed. It had barely been restored before the civil war broke out in 1922, and it was heavily damaged again. It's still a working post office today, although the small **Letters, Lives and Liberty Museum** does house a few diverting exhibits, including the original Declaration of Independence. That's all very much a secondary attraction, though; touching the bullet holes in the walls out front is a far more powerful way to experience a sense of this building's history. ○ *5 min. An Post, O'Connell St. www.anpost.ie.* ☎ *01/705-8833. Free admission. Counters open Mon–Sat 8:30am–6pm.*

❼ ★ Jim Larkin statue. You can almost hear "Big Jim" rallying the troops, bronze arms outstretched, in this work by Oisin Kelly (Garden of Remembrance, above).

Liverpool-born Larkin (1874–1947) founded the Irish Transport & General Workers' Union. This strong union threatened the bosses and members were forced to leave, leading to the great lockout of 1913, when 100,000 workers were sacked. The struggle continued for 8 months. The feisty Liverpudlian was the first leader of the Irish Labour party and continued campaigning for some of Ireland's poorest workers. ○ *5 min. O'Connell St., opposite the GPO.*

❽ ★★ Daniel O'Connell statue. Born into a Catholic family in 1775, O'Connell was a self-taught lawyer and politician and used his immense knowledge, influence, and political beliefs to change the life of Irish Catholics for good—no surprise that many called him "the Liberator.'" Previously, Irish Catholics were forbidden to vote, study, join professions, or stand for Parliament. Advocating nonviolent political reform, he was committed to their emancipation and formed the Catholic Association in 1823. A year after Parnell won election to the British Parliament—yet ironically unable to take a seat because of his religion—the Catholic Emancipation Act was passed, making O'Connell the uncrowned king of Ireland in many people's eyes (his crypt is a highlight in **Glasnevin Cemetery;** see ❾ below). Befitting his status, the statue stands at one of the city's most visible points. ○ *5 min. O'Connell St.*

❾ ★★ Glasnevin Cemetery & Museum. North of the city center, the Irish national cemetery was founded in 1832 and covers more than 50 hectares (124 acres). Most people buried here were ordinary citizens, but there are also many famous names on the headstones, ranging from former Irish Taoiseach (prime minister) Eamon de Valera to

O'Connell's tower in Glasnevin Cemetery.

other political heroes and rebels including Michael Collins, Daniel O'Connell, Countess Constance Markievicz, and Charles Stewart Parnell. Literary figures also have their place here—you can find writers Christy Brown (immortalized in the film *My Left Foot*) and Brendan Behan. A small museum is devoted to the cemetery and its famous occupants. Guided tours run daily, or you can download a self-guided tour app for your smartphone for €10 via the cemetery's website. Maps showing who's buried where are sold in the flower shop at the entrance. ⏱ *45 min. Finglas Rd., Glasnevin. www.glasnevintrust.ie.* ☎ *01/882-6550. Museum & tour €12 adults & seniors, €8 students & children, €25 families; museum only €6 adults, €4 seniors, students & children, €15 families. Museum: Mon–Fri 10am–5pm; Sat–Sun & public holidays 11am–5pm. Tours: Mon–Fri 11:30am & 2:30pm; Sat–Sun 10:30 & 11:30am, 12:30, 1:30 & 2:30pm. Bus: inc. 4, 9, 40.* ●

North of **Royal Canal**

The Best **Neighborhood Walks**

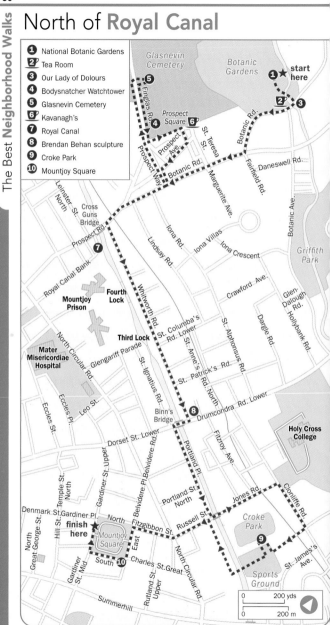

Previous page: Walking through the Liffey River neighborhood.

Off the beaten track, this walk takes in some of my Dublin favorites, including gardens, heroic history, and sporting prowess. Try to save it for a nice day, weather-wise, since it covers a large distance with few sheltering spots. Although the Northside is gaining in popularity these days, it's still fairly unfashionable; however, you'll come across one of the city's first prestigious Georgian squares. START: **Bus 13, 13A & 19 to Botanic Gardens.**

❶ ★★★ National Botanic Gardens.

Going strong for more than 200 years, these 20-hectare (50-acre) gardens house more than 20,000 species of rare and cultivated plants from around the world. Depending on the season, you might see rhododendrons, roses, vast conifers, or Chinese plants. The curvilinear wall is a real highlight: an immense glass house whose walls comprise more than 8,400 panes of glass. Guided tours (€5) take place Monday to Saturday at 11:30am and 3pm; and free tours are offered on Sunday at noon and 2:30pm. There are also regular exhibitions and talks in the Visitor Centre; check the website for upcoming events. ○ 1½ hr. Botanic Rd., Glasnevin. www.botanicgardens.ie. ☎ 01/804-0300. Free admission. Mar–Oct Mon–Fri 9am–5pm; Sat, Sun & public holidays 10am–6pm. Nov–Feb Mon–Fri 9am–4:30pm; Sat, Sun & public holidays 10am–4:30pm. Free tours Sun noon & 2:30pm. Bus: 83. 83A.

Greenhouse in National Botanic Gardens.

❷ Tea Room.

Located at the Visitor Centre, this is a pleasant spot for a cup of tea, a snack, or a light meal. *National Botanic Gardens.* ☎ 01-857 0909. $.

❸ ★ Our Lady of Dolours.

From a distance it looks like an ebony pyramid in the middle of a traffic circle…which is pretty much what it is, really. Constructed from dark timber, the **Pyramid Church** (its unofficial name) was built in 1972. Although the interior lacks ornate charm, etched-glass windows depict the 14 Stations of the Cross (Jesus's final hours before his crucifixion). ○ 15 min. Cnr. Botanic Ave. & Botanic Rd. ☎ 01/837-9445. Free admission. Daily around 9am–6:30pm. Bus: 4, 9, 83, 83A.

❹ ★★★ Bodysnatcher Watchtower.

As you walk around the cemetery's perimeter wall, you'll pass the watchtower on the

southwest corner. Here, watchmen would guard against bodysnatchers, or "sack-em-ups," who attempted to dig up fresh corpses to supply the medical profession for anatomy students. *Finglas Rd.*

5 ★★ Glasnevin Cemetery.
The cemetery brings the nation's history, ironically, to life. This vast burial ground, Ireland's largest, opened its gates in 1832 after Daniel O'Connell's efforts to allow Catholics the first chance to be buried in their own cemetery. Before that, the wealthy were buried in Protestant graveyards; the poor by the roadside. An estimated 1.5 million people lie here, half of them in unmarked graves. As well as ordinary people, luminaries from Ireland's history interred here include **Daniel O'Connell,** in a recently repainted crypt decorated with Celtic art; **Michael Collins,** whose grave is always covered with fresh flowers; **Charles Stuart Parnell** (see p 46, **5**), marked by a huge stone; former president **Eamon de Valera,** whose gravestone has often been vandalized; and **Bobby Sands** and the IRA hunger-strikers of the 1980s. Admire the stonework and ornate crosses as you pick your way through the rows. The daily tours by local historians are unmissable.

Brendan Behan statue.

There's a small but informative museum, or you can download a self-guided tour app for your smartphone for €10 via the cemetery's website. Maps showing who's buried where can be bought from the flower shop by the entrance.
🕐 *45 min. Finglas Rd., Glasnevin. See p 47,* **9**.

6 ★★ Kavanagh's. Better known by its grisly but appropriate nickname "The Gravediggers," this handsome Victorian pub has a good dining room attached. The urban legends about this place, involving wakes that go on for days–and coffins going unburied as a result–are legion. *1 Prospect Sq.* ☎ *01/830-7978. $.*

7 ★ Royal Canal. Join the canal from Prospect Road for a serene walk along its bank. Several locks along the way, still hand-operated, date back to the 1790s, and you'll usually see a fair smattering of ducks and the occasional swan. Peer over the high wall on your right to catch a glimpse of the infamous **Mountjoy Prison,** where Brendan Behan did time for his involvement in the planned assassination of two policemen in 1942. 🕐 *45 min to include Croke Park (**9**).*

8 ★★ Brendan Behan sculpture. Of Dublin's countless statues and sculptures, this is one of the best. Commissioned for what would have been Behan's 80th birthday in 2003, it commemorates the author of *Borstal Boy* (among other books), who was not only a great writer, but also a revolutionary (a bad one, by his own admission) and an immense drinker. A famous anecdote concerns an interview Behan once gave for Canadian television. "Why have you come to Canada?" he was asked. "Well now," he replied, "I was in a bar in

Ireland plays England at Croke Park.

Dublin, and it had one of those coasters. And it said, 'Drink Canada Dry,' so I thought I'd give it a shot." Alcoholism informed his legendary wit, but it also proved his undoing, and he died in 1964, aged just 41. Now, he sits on the bench talking to a pigeon, and for a former hellraiser, this peaceful setting never fails to raise a smile. After you pass the sculpture, cross Drumcondra Road and join the canal on its opposite bank. 🕐 *5 min.*

⑨ ★ Croke Park. It's hard to miss this mammoth stadium as you continue east along the canal. It's worth noting the extraordinary history of this sporting venue. Built by volunteers to promote Gaelic games, starting with initial meetings in 1884, Croke Park has played a major part in Irish nationalist history as host to Gaelic football and hurling matches for over a century. The **GAA Museum** does a good job of setting out the history of these games and putting them into the wider historical context of the importance of sport to the Irish way of life. 🕐 *45 min. Jones Rd. www. crokepark.ie.* ☎ *01/819-2300. Tour & museum: €12.50 adults; €9.50 seniors & students; €8.50 children under 12; €34–€38 families. Museum only: €6 adults; €5 seniors & students;* €4 children under 12; €16 families. Museum open Mon–Sat 9:30am–5pm; Sun 10:30am–5pm (June–Aug open Mon–Sat until 6pm); on match days, call to confirm hours. Tour times: July–Aug hourly 10am–4pm (10am–3pm Sun). Sept–June Mon–Fri 11am, 1, 3pm (also 4pm in June); Sat 10, 11am, noon, 1, 2, 3pm; Sun 11am, noon, 1, 2, 3pm (also 10am in June). On match days, call to confirm hours. Bus: inc. 1, 11, 13.

⑩ ★ Mountjoy Square. Although now decidedly more shabby than in its heyday, this area was the epitome of fashionable Dublin until well into the 19th century. It was originally known as Gardiner's Square, after its founder Luke Gardiner, and building began in 1792 in typical Georgian style: 18 houses on each side of a uniform square. Today, much of it has been converted into apartments. The south side of the square has altered the most, although the eastern side retains much of its original charm. Former residents include the great stuccodore Charles Thorpe (nos. 12 and 22), who worked on City Hall, and the writer Sean O'Casey, who rented a room at no. 35. From here, it's a 20-minute walk along Gardiner Place to reach O'Connell Street. 🕐 *20 min.*

Renewed Docklands

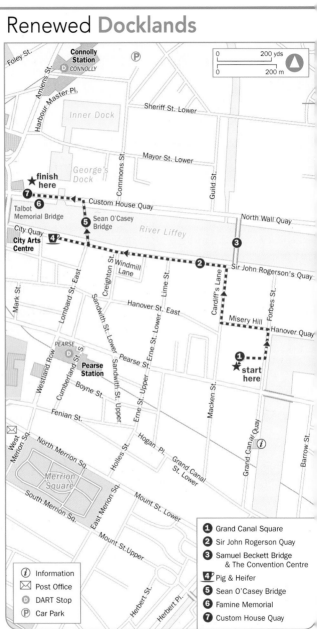

Connolly Station
CONNOLLY

Inner Dock

Sheriff St. Lower

Mayor St. Lower

George's Dock

★ finish here

Talbot Memorial Bridge

City Quay
City Arts Centre

Custom House Quay

Sean O'Casey Bridge

River Liffey

North Wall Quay

Windmill Lane

Hanover St. East

Sir John Rogerson's Quay

Misery Hill

Hanover Quay

★ start here

PEARSE

Pearse Station

Boyne St.

Fenian St.

Hogan Pl.

Grand Canal St. Lower

Merrion Square

North Merrion Sq.

West Merrion Sq.

South Merrion Sq.

East Merrion Sq.

Mount St. Lower

Mount St. Upper

Herbert St.

Herbert Pl.

0   200 yds
0   200 m

① Grand Canal Square
② Sir John Rogerson Quay
③ Samuel Beckett Bridge & The Convention Centre
④ Pig & Heifer
⑤ Sean O'Casey Bridge
⑥ Famine Memorial
⑦ Custom House Quay

ⓘ Information
✉ Post Office
Ⓓ DART Stop
Ⓟ Car Park

The old docklands of Dublin have been undergoing huge-scale regeneration since the 2000s. Now filled with glass-fronted apartments and wine bars, the city's focal point is shifting farther east–although, as of recently, many lie empty. You might want to explore the area during the slightly busier weekdays. START: **Bus 2, 3 & 77. DART: Grand Canal Dock.**

❶ ★★ Grand Canal Square.

The city's largest paved public square is a good point to observe the docks. Designed by top U.S. architect Martha Schwartz, the garden and concourse opened in 2007 with red paved walkways, giant red rods (somewhat redolent of glowing chopsticks), a water feature, and plants. Come back at night to see the "chopsticks" lit up and the gorgeous reflections on the still water. On the west side of the square, the uninspiringly-named **Bord Gáis Energy Theatre** (www. bordgaisenergytheatre.ie; ☎ 01/677-7999) opened in 2010. It hosts mostly big touring stage musicals. Meanwhile, **Surfdock** (www.surfdock.ie; ☎ 01/668-3945) offers taster windsurfing sessions for adults within the docks. It's located in an old Aran Islands Ferry on the docks' south side, accessed from Pearse St. ⏱ *30 min. Bus: inc. 1, 27, 47.*

Grand Canal Square and the Bord Gáis Energy Theatre.

❷ ★ Sir John Rogerson Quay.
The life-size iron sculpture *The Linesman* by Dony MacManus depicts a docker heaving in ropes,

Dublin docklands.

The striking Famine Memorial.

dragging something presumably extremely heavy given the look on his face. ⏱ *10 min.*

❸ ★ **Samuel Beckett Bridge & The Convention Centre.** San-tiago Calatrava's dramatic design, likened to a harp lying on its side, dominates the area and is the latest bridge to cross the Liffey. With four traffic lanes, cycle tracks, and foot-paths, it also opens at 90 degrees to enable ships to pass. It leads directly to the Convention Centre, a purpose-built international confer-ence venue, which even the keen-est architectural connoisseurs might liken to a slanted can of beans. ⏱ *10 min. Spencer Dock.*

4️⃣ ★ **Pig & Heifer.** One of the best places in the hood for a quick and tasty lunch, the Pig & Heifer claims to have been the first authentic New York–style delis in Dublin when it opened in the '90s—and they may well be right. There are also city center branches on Charlotte St., Amiens St., and Pearse St. *21–23 City Quay. www. pigandheifer.ie.* ☎ *01/633-6972. $.*

❺ ★ **Sean O'Casey Bridge.** Honoring the great Dublin writer (1880–1964), this was the third

bridge built over the Liffey since 2000. As you cross the 100m (110 yd) over the river, mutter to your-self, "The whole world is in a terri-ble state of chassis," from O'Casey's *Juno and the Paycock.* The bridge's slight sway no doubt prompted its local nickname "Quiver on the River" (which also relates to the Millennium or Mill Bridge, farther down the river). The graceful construction opens into two sections, swinging 90 degrees to allow tall boats to pass through. ⏱ *10 min.*

❻ ★★ **Famine Memorial.** This striking bronze series of sculptures commemorates the Great Famine of the mid–19th century, when Ire-land lost millions of people to star-vation and emigration. It's fitting that it stands here, on the very docks where so many desperate people fled on ships, mostly bound for the U.S. The memorial, created by Rowan Gillespie, was allegedly commissioned for Boston, Massa-chusetts, but their local mayor found it "too depressing"; hence it stayed right here. Depicting several hunger-ravaged people, plus a dog, the haunting image stands ironically in the shadow of the **International Financial Services Centre (IFSC)**, created by the government in 1987. The symbolism is harsh (intentionally?), given that this is the engine room of the modern Irish economy and contains half the world's top 50 banks–even taking into account the recent global recession. Amazing what changes occur in 150 years. ⏱ *10 min. Custom House Quay.*

❼ ★★ Custom House Quay (chq Building). Located in George's Dock, the **chq Building**, now transformed into a chic shopping center, has a fascinating history. Constructed in 1796 and designed by John Rennie, this was previously known as Stack A, built as a warehouse storing tobacco and tea, with vaults for wine, rum, and whiskey. On an unforgettable night in 1833, a devastating fire caused burning spirits to flow into the river, and it was noted that "the Liffey was a sheet of flame for half its breadth," visible for miles (and many lamenting the waste of good spirits along the way). In 1856 it

The chq Building, in Dublin's docklands, has a number of shops, cafes, and restaurants.

hosted the famous Crimean War Banquet to honor Irish troops who served in a war that suffered some 750,000 casualties. In the mall that lies there today, you can still see the original elements of the roof. ⏱ *30 min. Docklands. www.chq.ie. Mon–Fri 7am–7pm; Sat 10am–6pm.*

Liffey **Boardwalk**

Legend:
- (i) Information
- ⊠ Post Office
- Ⓓ DART Stop
- Ⓟ Car Park

start here ①

② Ormond Quay

③ Enoteca delle Langhe

④ Four Courts

⑤ St. Michan's Church

⑦ ⑥ finish here

St. Mary's Pro Cathedral

Rotunda Hosp.

Gate Theatre

Gardens of Remembrance

Parnell Sq. East

Parnell Sq. West

Police Station

Moore St.

Henry St.

O'Connell St. Lower

O'Connell St. Upper

Thomas's Ln.

Cathedral St.

Earl St. North

Abbey St. Lower

Eden Quay

O'Connell Bridge

Burgh Quay

Hawkins St.

D'Olier St.

Westmoreland St.

College St.

Pearse St.

Tara St. Ⓓ

TARA ST. Ⓓ

Poolbeg St.

Trinity College

College Park

Nassau St.

Suffolk St.

Wicklow St.

Exchequer St.

Andrew's St.

College Green

(i)

Bank of Ireland

Fowne's St.

Cope St.

Fleet St.

Temple Bar

TEMPLE BAR

Aston Quay

Ha'penny Bridge

Bachelor's Walk

Lotts

Abbey St. Middle

Abbey St. Upper

Liffey St.

River Liffey

Wellington Quay

Essex Quay

Temple Ln. S.

Dame St.

Parliament Sq.

(i)

Lord Edward St.

Castle St.

Dublin Castle

Christ Church ✝

St. Werburgh's ✝

Princess St.

Strand St. Great

Ormond Quay Upper

Ormond Quay

Grattan Bridge

Wood Quay

Exch. Quay

Essex Quay Lwr.

Cook St.

St. Audoen's ✝

High St.

Merchant's Quay

Bridge St. Upp.

Thomas St. West

Cornmarket

St. James's Gate Guinness Brewery

Jervis St.

Mary St.

Mary's Abbey

Capel St.

Arran St. East

George's Hill

Mary's Lane

Chancery Pl.

Charles St.

St. Michan's St.

Ann St. North

Greek St.

Beresford St.

Coleraine St.

Green St.

College of Tech.

Dominick St. Lower

Dominick St. Upper

Dorset St. Upper

King's Inns

North Bolton St.

Granby Row

Parnell St.

Church St. Upp Constitution Hill

North King St.

Bow St.

May Lane

Lincoln Lane

Court House

Inns Quay

Church St.

Smithfield

The Chimney

Blackhall Pl.

Blackhall St.

Queen St.

Brunswick St. North

Grangegorman Lower

Stoney Batter

Kirwan St.

Arbour Hill

Benburb St.

Barsfield Quay

Esplanade

Ellis Quay

Usher's Island

Usher's Quay

Arran Quay

Oliver Bond St.

Bridgefoot St.

Watling St.

Wolfe Tone Quay

Victoria Quay

Barsfield Quay

N ▲

0   200 yds

0   200 m

Created as part of a huge reconstruction project around the turn of the Millennium, the Liffey Boardwalk is a good starting point to explore the river's traffic-free north bank. Even considering the city's high rainfall, it's no surprise that the river has never flooded, given the immensely high river wall built in 1800. We start with the imposing historic landmark Custom House, ending at one of the city's finest museums. START: **Bus 53A to Custom House Quay or 15, 45 & 65 to Eden Quay. LUAS: Busáras.**

❶ ★★ Custom House. You'll be hard pushed to miss this glorious building, dominating the north quay and architecturally one of Dublin's most important landmarks. Designed by Englishman James Gandon and completed in 1791, this beautifully proportioned building has a long classical facade of graceful pavilions, arcades, and a central dome topped by a statue of Commerce. The 14 keystones over the doors and windows are known as the Riverine Heads, because they represent the Atlantic Ocean and the 13 principal rivers of Ireland. Although it burned to a shell in 1921, the building has been masterfully restored. Take a good look at Hibernia, seen embracing Britannia while Neptune drives away famine and despair. It was located on this part of the quay in an attempt to shift the city's center slightly

farther east, which angered city merchants at the time. Gaze at this scene at night from the south side of the river, or get up close from around the back through the parking lot ⏱ *20 min. Luas: Busáras. Bus: inc. 27C, 41X, 53A.*

❷ ★ Ormond Quay. Walking west along the Boardwalk, you'll come to the loveliest example of recent developments in the area. Walk past the famous Ha'penny Bridge (p 14, ❻), and the *Hags with the Bags* sculpture–two ladies resting on a bench complete with Arnotts shopping bags. You'll then come to the quaint Italian quarter, **Quartier Bloom,** a tiny enclave of eateries with outdoor tables nestled around a cozy alleyway, complete with a huge mural of The Last Supper on the outside wall. It adds a Mediterranean ambience to the place, where locals love to pop in

The beautifully proportioned Custom House on the Liffey River.

St. Michan's Church crypt.

for lunch or a coffee, or to stock up on Italian foodstuffs. ⏱ *10 min.*

3 ★★ **Enoteca delle Langhe.** This cozy wine bar and restaurant is popular with local workers. Their antipasti and sharing plates make for a particularly good lunchtime nibble. *Blooms Lane. www.wallace winebars.ie. ☎ 01/888-0834. $$$.*

4 ★★ **Four Courts.** A Dublin landmark with its large drum-shaped roof topped by a shallow dome, this building originally held the four divisions that made up the

Ormond Quay and Ha'Penny Bridge.

judicial system. Designed by James Gandon (see also **1**), its imposing exterior is enhanced by Edward Smyth's sculptures, with Moses flanked by Justice and Mercy on the main pediment. Destroyed by fire during the Civil War of 1921, the building was restored with few changes to the exterior. ⏱ *15 min.* See p 21, **7**.

5 ★★ **St. Michan's Church.** Around the corner, St. Michan's is the oldest parish church on the Northside, dating back to 1095 when it served the Viking invaders. Pop in to see the original organ on which (legend has it) Handel practiced for his first performance of the *Messiah*. Also on show is the original 1720s piece of carved oak depicting 17 musical instruments. Descend the steep stone steps to see the vaults, wherein lie St. Michan's decidedly unique attraction: mummified bodies, in open coffins—their rather alarming state of preservation having something to do with the atmosphere. It's creepy enough to (allegedly) have once inspired a love of the macabre in a young writer by the name of Bram Stoker. ⏱ *45 min. Church St., Dublin 7. See p 20,* **6**.

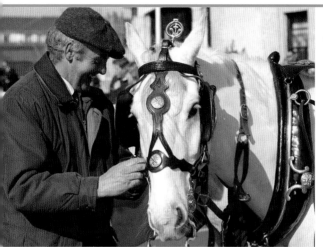

The Horse Market at Smithfield.

❻ ★ Smithfield. From the church, turn left and cut through May Lane. Smithfield is the original wide cobbled street where horses and cattle have traded since 1664. The traditional **Horse Market**, Europe's largest, still takes place in Smithfield Square on the first Sundays of March and September, attracting travelers and villagers from all over Ireland. The rest of the month it's a peaceful urban retreat with modern studio apartments and tasteful street lighting. It also hosts the occasional concert, Christmas market, and ice-rink in winter. ⏱ *40 min.*

❼ ★ The Old Jameson Distillery. Learn as much as you can bear about one of Ireland's most famous whiskies from the right-in-front-of-your-eyes demonstrations at this working distillery on the north side of the city. At the conclusion of the tour, you can sip a little firewater and see what you think. A couple of lucky people on each tour are selected to be "tasters" and sample different Irish, Scotch, and American whiskeys. Tours run throughout the day, about every 30 minutes, and last an hour. You can get a 10% discount by booking online. ⏱ *1 hr. Bow St. www.jameson whiskey.com.* ☎ *01/807-2348. Admission €15 adults; €12 seniors 7 students; €8 children; €40 families. Mon–Sat 9am–6pm; Sun 10am–6pm; last tours 5:15pm. No alcohol sold on Sun after 12:30pm. Bus: inc. 67, 68, 69.*

Old Jameson Distillery.

Around Temple Bar

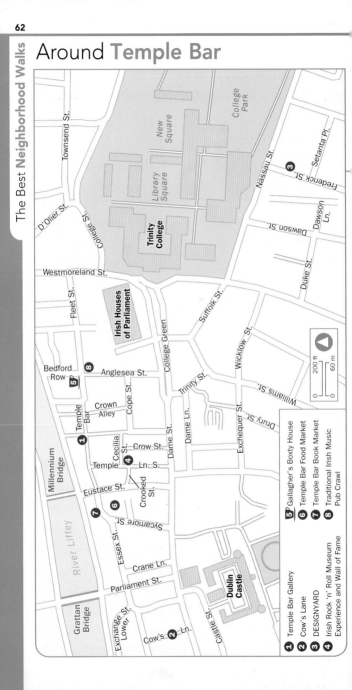

1 Temple Bar Gallery
2 Cow's Lane
3 DESIGNYARD
4 Irish Rock 'n' Roll Museum Experience and Wall of Fame
5 Gallagher's Boxty House
6 Temple Bar Food Market
7 Temple Bar Book Market
8 Traditional Irish Music Pub Crawl

Explore this warren of narrow cobblestone streets along the Liffey by day when it's peaceful and clear of nocturnal bar-hoppers who are still at home, nursing hangovers from the night before. Confusingly, Temple Bar is the name both of the district and its main thoroughfare, which is mostly pedestrianized. Saturdays are best of all, when several colorful markets draw treasure seekers and bargain hunters in droves: the book market on Temple Bar Square, the food market on Meeting House Square, and the Designer Mart on Cow's Lane. START: **Bus 15, 15a, 50 & 77 to College Street.**

① ★★ Temple Bar Gallery. This wonderful gallery and artists-in-residence studio sums up all that's appealing about Temple Bar: lively, edgy, contemporary, and always with something interesting to see. Some of Ireland's most cutting-edge contemporary artists have had their work shown here, and you can even book a slot (for free) to see artists at work. The gallery hosts talks and other special events regularly; see the website for details. ⏱ 1½ hr. 5–9 Temple Bar. See p 21, **⑧**.

② ★★ Cow's Lane. This little street at the edge of Temple Bar is filled with bijou boutiques carrying the latest Irish fashion designs, beautiful fabrics, and adorable handbags. Among the cream of the crop is **Claire Garvey** at no. 6

(www.clairegarvey.com; ☎ 01/671-7287). A superstar in the Irish fashion world, Claire's elegant and dramatic creations have been wowing fashionistas since the mid-2000s. Come on Saturday between 10am and 5pm to browse the open-air fashion market, **DesignerMart**, where cut-rate bargains are often found. ⏱ 45 min.

③ ★★★ DESIGNyard. This is the kind of place that's irresistible to browse, even if you've no intention of buying anything. Many of Ireland's leading jewelry designers have pieces for sale here, and prices are pretty steep accordingly–although you can usually find some more affordable, quality items for around €100. If you're planning to get hitched, this is also considered one of the best places in the

Temple Bar Gallery.

A hat stall at Cow's Lane Market.

country to buy engagement rings. ⓒ *20 min. 25 S. Frederick St. www. designyard.ie.* ☎ *01/474-1011. Tues–Wed, Fri 10am–5:30pm; Thurs 10am–8pm; Sat 10am–6pm. Closed Sun & Mon.*

④ ★ **Irish Rock 'n Roll Museum Experience and Wall of Fame.** Not so much a museum as a tour of a demo studio with a few exhibits thrown in, the Rock 'n Roll Museum opened to some fanfare in 2015. The tour culminates with the chance to form a "band" with your fellow visitors and lay down a track in the studio. Exhibits on display include vintage instruments and assorted memorabilia, such a blank check signed by Bono for an autograph hunter. Outside,

on Curved Street, is the **Irish Music Wall of Fame**, where giant photographic portraits of Ireland's top music stars, including Van Morrison, U2, and the Cranberries, adorn one side of the building. ⓒ *1 hr. (museum);* ⓒ *5 min (wall). Curved St., off Temple Bar.* ☎ *01/635-1993. Tours (must be prebooked) €16 adults; €14 seniors, students & children 12–17; €12 children under 12; €50 families. Daily 10am–5:30pm.*

⑤ ★★★ **Gallagher's Boxty House.** Traditional Irish cooking has had a real renaissance in the last few years, as a new generation rediscovers and reclaims the old culinary traditions of this island. And this fantastic (and super cool) restaurant, smack dab in the middle of Temple Bar, is one of its best proponents. A must. *20–21 Temple Bar. www.boxtyhouse.ie.* ☎ *01/677-2762. $$.*

⑥ ★ **Temple Bar Food Market.** Every Saturday, the small Meeting House Square fills with the irresistible odors of street food sizzling in pans and woks and over hot coals. The lines can stretch almost half the way back down to Temple Bar at lunchtime. Stalls also sell fresh pastries, cakes, cheeses, fruits

Temple Bar Food Market.

Pub crawl music.

and veggies, and a range of other products–so this is a great place to stock up for picnic foods too. The market takes place directly in front of **Filmbase** (see p 129), which usually has some intriguing contemporary art in the lobby. Its opening times are erratic, but never mind— the glass walls mean you can enjoy the art while chowing down on whatever irresistible snack you've just picked up. Note also the colorful, surrealist mural, high on the wall of the building opposite. ○ *20 min. Meeting House Sq. Sat 10am–4:30pm.*

⑦ ★ Temple Bar Book Market. Another charming little open-air market, this is the place to come and browse for secondhand books. What you'll find is anybody's guess; the selection is usually quite small, but surprisingly varied. You might well discover some rare titles or first editions, however, and it will come as no surprise at all that books by Irish writers are particularly well represented. There's usually a good selection of children's books as well. The market takes place every weekend. ○ *20 min. Temple Bar Square. Sat–Sun 10am–6pm.*

⑧ ★★ Traditional Irish Music Pub Crawl. These lively walking tours are led by two professional musicians, who sing as you make your way through Temple Bar, stopping at one musical pub and another. In between entertaining you with their impressive performing skills, your guides tell you some of the history of Irish music and its profound influence around the world. Each pub you stop at has a private area set aside, so you won't have to squeeze in among all the other patrons (a good thing too, as Temple Bar pubs get *seriously* busy from early evening onwards—and sometimes all day). All the pubs are quite close together, so you shouldn't have to wear your best walking shoes to take part. However, no kids are allowed. Tours meet at 7:30pm, upstairs at **Oliver St. John Gogarty's** pub, on the corner of Fleet Street and Anglesea Street. You can book in advance or buy tickets on the night. ○ *2 hr. www.discoverdublin.ie/musical-pub-crawl.* ☎ *01/475-3313. Tickets €12 adults; € 10 students. Apr–Oct daily 7:30pm; Nov–Mar Thurs–Sat 7:30pm.*

Grand Canal **to Portobello**

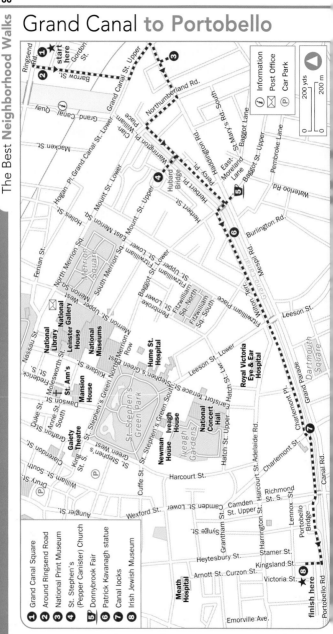

- ① **Information**
- ⊠ **Post Office**
- Ⓟ **Car Park**

0 — 200 yds
0 — 200 m

① Grand Canal Square
② Around Ringsend Road
③ National Print Museum
④ St. Stephen's (Pepper Canister) Church
⑤ Donnybrook Fair
⑥ Patrick Kavanagh statue
⑦ Canal locks
⑧ Irish Jewish Museum

This tour starts at Grand Canal Square, twinned with the U.K.'s huge Grand Union Canal, and follows the canal west, with a couple of detours. It ends in redbrick, terraced Portobello, once a working-class area and home to most of the city's Jewish community—including Leopold Bloom, the fictional Jewish hero in Joyce's *Ulysses*. START: **Bus 2, 3 & 77.** DART: **Grand Canal Dock.**

❶ ★ Grand Canal Square.

Enjoy the expanse of the paved concourse, hub of the re-created Docklands area. Peek into the courtyard around the back of the Millennium Tower in Charlotte Quay, and you'll see an amusing and unusual exhibit: a huge concrete model of a letter, written by William Jessop, designer of the docks that opened in 1776, to the Board of the Grand Canal Co. In it, he complains about a wall that was "shoving out at the foot and spoiling from the backing," which Jessop felt was "in consequence of the piles not having been driven with a sufficient batter." His ire is audible, even after all these years. *See p 55*, ❶.

❷ ★ Around Ringsend Road.

As you emerge onto Ringsend Road, to the right you'll see the seven-floor, stone **Trinity Technology and Enterprise Campus**, a restored sugar refinery dating back to 1862 and now housing artisans' studios (visitors welcome). Opposite is what remains of **Bolands Flour Mills** (now derelict) where Eamon de Valera was in charge of the troops during the 1916 Easter Rising. This was one of several strategic points in the city the rebels used as bases; the mills covered the docks, where any troops sent to Dublin would disembark. Nearby Barrow and South Dock streets have swaths of construction and glass apartment blocks, but you can still glimpse the original terraces down Gordon Street, towards the old gas station.

❸ ★ National Print Museum.

This surprisingly absorbing little museum displays printing presses, machinery, and other assorted artifacts from an industry that seems so distant in today's digital world that it may as well be medieval. Until very recently the museum had one of the few remaining original copies of the 1916 Proclamation of Independence, although there's plenty of other diverting prints and historic newspapers. They also run workshops and other special events—check the website for details. The museum, which is deliberately styled like a print shop from the 1930s or '40s, is located in what was once the Garrison chapel of a former army barracks. ⏱ *40 min. Garrison Chapel, Beggar's Bush, Haddington Rd. www.nationalprintmuseum.ie.* ☎ *01/660-3770. Admission €4 adults; €3 seniors, students & children; €8 families. Mon–Fri*

National Print Museum.

9am–5pm; Sat–Sun 2–5pm; closed public holiday weekends. DART: Grand Canal Dock.

④ ★ St. Stephen's (Pepper Canister) Church. Walk over the quaint **Huband Bridge,** built in 1791 and the canal's most ornate bridge. Take a detour and turn right up to St. Stephen's Church, nicknamed the Pepper Canister because of the shape of its dome. An Anglican church, this was the last of a series of Georgian churches established by the Church of Ireland and built in the suburbs as the population expanded. The church stands on Mount Street Crescent, the name of which is thought to derive from the mound that once stood at the corner of Fitzwilliam and Baggot streets, where gallows were used for executions. Sadly the church is open intermittently at best—either for a service (usually 11am on the first Sunday of the month only) or a concert. There's often a free classical-music recital at Thursday lunchtime; check the website for the full schedule of what's coming up. Outside the church, look for Derek Fitzsimon's charming sculptures of children that line the square. ○ *15 min. Mount St. Cres.*

Riding bikes by St. Stephen's Church.

www.peppercanister.ie. ☎ 01/288-0663. *Services first Sun of the month only, 11am.*

⑤ Donnybrook Fair. There are cafes all along Baggot Street; one of the best is Donnybrook Fair, an excellent deli and bakery. If the weather's fine, grab supplies here and head to one of the benches along the canal for an impromptu picnic. *13 Baggot St.* ☎ *01/668-3556. $.*

⑥ ★★ Patrick Kavanagh statue. Located on the north bank, this charming life-size sculpture of poet Patrick Kavanagh (1905–67) sits on a bench, acknowledging his wish, "Oh commemorate me where there is water." Like his drinking buddy Brendan Behan, whose statue sits along Royal Canal (see p 52, ⑦), Kavanangh is remembered in a tranquil location rather than his (and Behan's) favorite bar, McDaid's.

⑦ ★ Canal locks. Walking along the canal's north bank you may be lucky enough to see a boat coming through the locks, all seven of which are operated manually by lock-keepers. The last commercial

Playing by the canal locks.

barge chugged through here in 1950, but with ongoing renovation by the Inland Waterways Association of Ireland there has been an increase in canal transport, mainly for leisure. Once you reach **Portobello Bridge** (also called Le Touche), peer south down Rathmines Road to the immense pale green dome of the Church of Mary Immaculate Refuge of Sinners. Lush weeping willow trees dip into the canal's waters, where you'll also see Portobello College. On the right, redbrick terraces line the quaint, narrow streets.

⑧ ★★ Irish Jewish Museum.

Portobello was once a thriving center for the small Jewish community in Ireland, and while it's no longer a particularly Jewish area, it makes a

fitting home for this small but interesting museum. The diaspora reaches further than you might think—for example, Chaim Herzog, President of Israel from 1983 to 1993, was born in Ireland, and lived in Portobello from 1919 to 1935. Exhibits going back to the mid-Victorian age tell the story of Jewish communities in Ireland, particularly in Dublin, Belfast, Limerick, Cork, and Derry. The rather unassuming museum building was constructed in 1917—you can view the original synagogue upstairs. ⏱ *45 min. 3 Walworth Rd. www.jewishmuseum. ie/.org/museum.html.* ☎ *085/706-7357. Free admission; donations welcome. May–Sept Sun, Tues & Thurs 11am–3pm; Oct–Apr Sun 10:30am–2:30pm. Bus: inc. 9, 16, 68.*

The Best Neighborhood Walks

Kilmainham to **Phoenix Park**

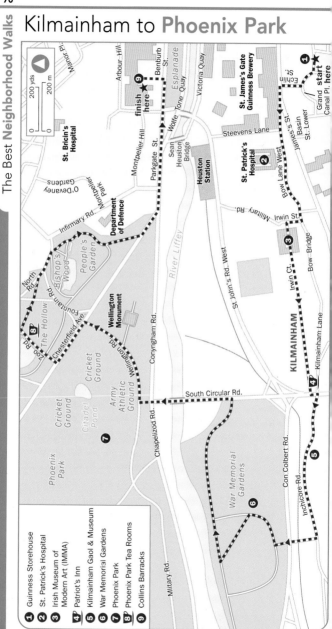

200 yds
200 m

Arbour Hill
Manor Pl.
Benburb St.
finish here 9
St. Bricin's Hospital
Esplanade
Victoria Quay
Wolfe Tone Quay
Sean Heuston Bridge
Montpelier Hill
Parkgate St.
Steevens Lane
St. James's Gate **Guinness Brewery**
James's St.
Echlin St.
start here 1
Grand Canal Pl.
Basin St. Lower
St. Patrick's Hospital 2
Bow Lane West
Heuston Station
Military Rd.
Irwin St.
3
O'Devaney Gardens
Infirmary Rd.
Montpelier Park
People's Garden
Department of Defence
Bishop's Wood
North Rd.
The Hollow
Zoo Rd.
Fountain Rd.
Chesterfield Ave.
8
River Liffey
St. John's Rd. West
Bow Bridge
KILMAINHAM
Irwin Ct.
Kilmainham Lane
4
Wellington Monument
Conyngham Rd.
Wellington Rd.
Cricket Ground
Cricket Ground
Citadel Pond
Army Athletic Ground
7
Phoenix Park
South Circular Rd.
Chapelizod Rd.
Con Colbert Rd.
Inchicore Rd.
5
War Memorial Gardens
6
Miltary Rd.

1 Guinness Storehouse
2 St. Patrick's Hospital
3 Irish Museum of Modern Art (IMMA)
4 Patriot's Inn
5 Kilmainham Gaol & Museum
6 War Memorial Gardens
7 Phoenix Park
8 Phoenix Park Tea Rooms
9 Collins Barracks

A prison, park, hospital, and barracks—plus areas rarely visited. Starting at the land of Guinness, this takes you through Kilmainham where Vikings settled 2,000 years ago, and home to the historic Gaol. After a peaceful walk to bucolic Phoenix Park, take in Collins Barracks' exhibitions if you have the energy. START: Bus 51B, 78A and 123 to James's Street.

❶ ★ Guinness Storehouse.

Absorbing even if you're not a lover of the "black stuff," this working brewery has been a fixture in this part of Dublin for more than 250 years. Arthur Guinness, the firm's eponymous founder, was born in Thomas Street, just around the corner; today his brewery is the center of a worldwide industry (although this is only one of several places in which the drink is actually made these days). Among the attractions to explore here is an appealing gallery devoted to the art of Guinness advertising—which anybody who's even set foot in an Irish theme pub will already be familiar with. Don't miss the **Gravity Bar,** on the top floor—the views across Dublin, in a 360-degree panorama, are nothing short of spectacular. ⏱ 1½ hr. St. James's Gate, off Robert St. See p 20, ❹.

❷ ★ St. Patrick's Hospital.

Walking down Bow Lane West, you can peek into the grounds of the hospital, financed by Jonathan Swift and opened in 1757. Then the Dean of St. Patrick's Cathedral and governor of the city workhouse, the man better known for penning children's classic *Gulliver's Travels* was at the forefront in treating the mentally ill. This was seen to be the most enlightened institution in the British Isles, for the first time treating the mentally ill as patients rather than criminals. Still operating as a psychiatric hospital, you can see the facade of his original building, designed by architect George Semple, from the southeast corner, although it doubled in size in 1778 with Thomas Cooley's additions. ⏱ 5 min. James's St.

❸ ★★ Irish Museum of Modern Art. This excellent center for

Tour of the Guinness Storehouse.

Kilmainham Gaol.

contemporary art is full of surprises. The permanent collection has more than 3,500 works, dating mostly from the 1940s to the present day. The grounds are also used to display art, which effectively turns them into another gallery. The museum is situated in the former Royal Hospital Kilmainham building; dating from 1684, it is considered to be one of the finest 17th-century buildings extant in Ireland. ⏱ *1 hr. Royal Hospital, Military Rd., Kilmainham, Dublin 8. See p 19,* ②.

War Memorial Gardens.

4 ★ **Patriot's Inn.** Right across from Kilmainham Gaol (see below), this pub serves decent bar food and snacks. The name is a reference to the Irish revolutionaries who were imprisoned at the gaol. *760 S. Circular Rd., Kilmainham.* ☎ *01/679-9595. $.*

5 ★★★ **Kilmainham Gaol.** Equal parts memorial and exhibition, this is an extremely powerful place to visit for anyone interested in the Irish struggle for independence from British rule. Many prominent revolutionaries were imprisoned here in the 19th and early 20th centuries. Many were also executed, including the leaders of the 1916 Easter Rising (one of them, James Connolly, broke his foot during the fighting, and so was shot while sitting down). It wasn't just political prisoners who suffered here; leaders of the suffragette movement also found themselves doing time in the grim cells, not to mention a roll call of notorious murderers and criminals. ⏱ *2 hr. Inchicore Rd. See p 19,* ①.

Bloom Festival in Phoenix Park.

6 ★ **War Memorial Gardens.**
Turn right onto Memorial Road and cross the busy Con Colbert Road to enter the peaceful gardens designed by Sir Edwin Lutyens and opened in 1939. The memorial commemorates more than 49,000 Irishmen killed in action during World War I, their names recorded in the granite bookrooms. The gardens are a delight to wander around, with surprisingly few people visiting the fragrant rose garden, fountains, and lily ponds. Walk towards the north, and when you hit the Liffey, turn right and keep walking—you'll pass the **University Boat House** and then **hurling grounds.** (There is a lovely walk if you turn left at the river, although lone visitors may find it too deserted.) At the exit gates, take the righthand fork, then turn left onto South Circular Road.

7 ★★ **Phoenix Park.** You may have already explored the huge park—at 700 hectares (1,730 acres), one of the world's largest—with its myriad attractions. It's the site of Áras un Uachtaráin (the President's Residence); a giant, 40-ton Papal Cross erected for Pope John Paul II's visit on 1979; an opulent estate that was once home to the fabled Guinness family; and great expanses of blooming flower gardens and sports fields. Look for cricket, hurling, and polo matches. The park is even home to the Dublin Zoo, which traces its roots back to 1831 and is the country's largest zoo. A new exhibit, the Sea Lion Cove, opened in 2015, introducing a frisky colony of California sea lions to the zoo. You'll enter the park near the huge **Wellington Monument** obelisk, so either cut through and exit via Park Gate, take time to explore and spot deer, or rent a bicycle (see p 98). If you don't have the time or energy, pop into the nearby **People's Garden** with its Victorian layout (p 98, **10**). 🕐 *1 hr. See "Phoenix Park" section in chapter 5.*

8 ★ **Phoenix Park Tea Rooms.**
This welcome cafe serves sandwiches, cakes, light snacks, and ice creams. There's a large seating area outside, which makes for a lovely place to recharge with a cup of tea when the sun is shining. *Opp entrance to Dublin Zoo, Phoenix Park.* ☎ *01-671 4431. $.*

Horse and carriage ride through Phoenix Park by Wellington Monument.

⑨ ★★ Collins Barracks. Built in 1702, this impressive building now houses the **National Museum: Decorative Arts and History**—one of four sites that collectively make up the National Museum of Ireland. It was still in use by the military until 1997. The collection focuses on history through decorative arts, such as fashion, furniture, and glassware.

Although most of the collection dates from the mid–18th century onwards, prized items in the permanent collection include the so-called Fonthill vase—the oldest known example of Chinese porcelain to have reached Europe, which it did as a gift to Pope Benedict XII in 1368. ⏱ *2 hr. Benburb St. See p 19,* ❸. ●

Collins Barracks.

Shopping Best Bets

Best **Bargain-Hunting for Fashionistas**
★★★ Om Diva, *27 Drury St. (p 83)*

Best **Streetwear for Well-heeled Teens**
★ BT2, *28–29 Grafton St. (p 82)*

Best for **Street Food**
★★ Temple Bar Food Market, *Meeting House Square (p 88)*

Best for **Exclusive Accessories**
★★★ Louise Kennedy, *56 Merrion Square (p 83)*

Danker Antiques. Previous page: Om Diva shop.

DANKER ANTIQUES

Best for **Handmade Engagement Rings**
★★★ DESIGNyard, *48–49 Nassau St. (p 86)*

Best for **Full-On Foodies**
★★★ Fallon & Byrne, *11–17 Exchequer St. (p 84)*

Best for **Knitted Homewares**
★★ Avoca, *11–13 Suffolk St. (p 85)*

Best for **Serious Bibliophiles**
★★★ Ulysses Rare Books, *10 Duke St. (p 80)*

Best for **Traditional Irish Penny Whistles**
★★ Waltons, *69 South Great George's St. (p 88)*

Most **Classy Department Store**
★★★ Brown Thomas, *88–95 Grafton St. (p 81)*

Best for **Contemporary Irish Art**
★★★ The Doorway Gallery, *24 S. Frederick St. (p 80)*

Best for **Last-Minute Souvenirs**
★ House of Ireland, *38 Nassau St. (p 85)*

Best for **Chocoholics**
★★ Butlers Chocolate Café, *51A Grafton St. (p 84)*

Around Grafton & Nassau Streets Shopping

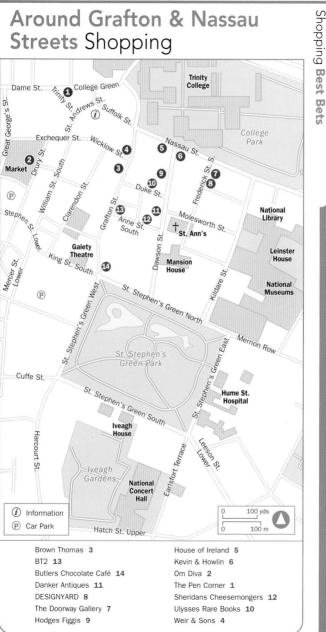

Brown Thomas **3**
BT2 **13**
Butlers Chocolate Café **14**
Danker Antiques **11**
DESIGNYARD **8**
The Doorway Gallery **7**
Hodges Figgis **9**

House of Ireland **5**
Kevin & Howlin **6**
Om Diva **2**
The Pen Corner **1**
Sheridans Cheesemongers **12**
Ulysses Rare Books **10**
Weir & Sons **4**

Dublin Shopping

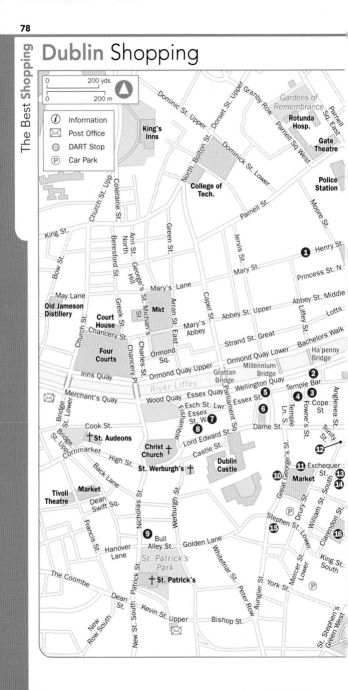

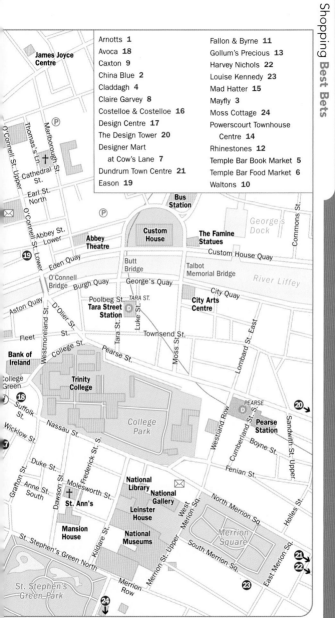

Arnotts **1**
Avoca **18**
Caxton **9**
China Blue **2**
Claddagh **4**
Claire Garvey **8**
Costelloe & Costelloe **16**
Design Centre **17**
The Design Tower **20**
Designer Mart
   at Cow's Lane **7**
Dundrum Town Centre **21**
Eason **19**

Fallon & Byrne **11**
Gollum's Precious **13**
Harvey Nichols **22**
Louise Kennedy **23**
Mad Hatter **15**
Mayfly **3**
Moss Cottage **24**
Powerscourt Townhouse
   Centre **14**
Rhinestones **12**
Temple Bar Book Market **5**
Temple Bar Food Market **6**
Waltons **10**

Dublin Shopping A to Z

Antiques & Art

★★ Caxton CITY CENTER

Antique prints from the 16th, 17th, and 18th centuries are a specialty of this wonderful art store. (In 2012, someone even identified a lost Renaissance masterpiece among the stock.) The prices can be astronomical, but even if you're not buying, browsing here is like being a kid in a candy store for lovers of the antiquarian. *63 Patrick St.* ☎ *01/453-0060. Map p 78.*

★ Christy Bird CITY CENTER

"VARIETY IS OUR SPECIALTY" proclaims a sign at this appealing antiques store, which has been in business since the 1940s. And it certainly lives up to the promise, stocked with a happy jumble of knick-knacks, collectibles, tat, and genuine antiques. The joy is that you never quite know what you're going to find. *32 S. Richmond St. www.christybird.com.* ☎ *01/475-4049.*

★★ Danker Antiques GRAF-

TON STREET This friendly, approachable dealer, in an arcade just off Dawson Street, has a fine collection of antique silver

tableware and jewelry. It specializes in designs from the Celtic Revival period of the early 20th century, and usually has some beautiful Art Deco pieces too. *1 4–5 Royal Hibernian Way. www.dankerantiques.com.* ☎ *01/677-4009. Map p 77.*

★★★ The Doorway Gallery

COLLEGE GREEN A mixture of new and established Irish artists display their work at this cheerful art gallery. There's always something wonderful to discover, and many prices are affordable too. *24 S. Frederick St. www.thedoorwaygallery.com.* ☎ *01/764-5895. Map p 77.*

★★ Green on Red SPENCER

DOCK Outstanding contemporary art can be found at this little gallery in the docklands, about a mile northwest of the city center. It has a dozen or so exhibitions per year. *Spencer Dock. www.theoriel.com.* ☎ *01/671-3414.*

Books & Stationery
★★★ Ulysses Rare Books

GRAFTON STREET When lovers of Irish literature and antiquarian books die, if they've been good,

The Doorway Gallery.

Hodges Figgis bookstore.

by the Waterstones chain, Hodges Figgis one of the go-to places in the city for books of all kinds. *56–58 Dawson St.* ☎ *01/677-4754. Map p 77.*

★★★ The Pen Corner COL-LEGE GREEN

Keeping the flame alive for the dying art of letter writing, this place is an utter delight. The Pen Corner sells exquisite fountain pens, paper, and other writing implements. They also stock beautiful notebooks and cards. *12 College Green. www.nobleandbeg-garmanbooks.com.* ☎ *01/679-3641. Map p 77.*

Department Stores

★★ Arnotts O'CONNELL STREET

Ireland's original department store, Arnott's first opened its illustrious doors in 1843. Its selection of womenswear, menswear, gifts, and beauty products is enormous. Weary shoppers will also be delighted to find a branch of that most famous of Dublin coffeehouses, Bewley's, next to the Abbey Street entrance on the lower ground floor. Arnott's stays open for late shopping until 9pm on Thursdays and 8pm on Fridays. *12 Henry St. www.arnotts.ie.* ☎ *01/805-0400. Map p 78.*

★★★ Brown Thomas GRAF-TON STREET

The top-hatted doorman out front sets a deceptively formal tone for this great old Dublin institution; we've always found it a relaxed and friendly place, even if the credit card seems to take a bit of a beating. Stop by for most of the major fashion labels before getting your nails done, having a one-to-one at the cosmetics counters, or indulging yourself at the bar and cafe or the elegant restaurant. *88–95 Grafton St. www. brownthomas.com.* ☎ *01/605-6666. Map p 77.*

they get to spend eternity at Ulysses Rare Books. This is where to come for rare copies of Joyce, Yeats, Wilde, Behan, Stoker, and just about every luminary of the Irish canon you can think of. Prices range from the barely affordable (€375 for a rare 1927 *Dracula*), to the stratospheric (€35,000 for a first-edition *Ulysses*) but it's simply heaven to browse. *10 Duke St.* ☎ *www.rarebooks.ie. 01/671-8676. Map p 77.*

★ Eason O'CONNELL STREET

This multi-story bookstore on O'Connell Street is one of Ireland's oldest, having been in business since 1819. Pretty much everything you could want is here, from history and local-interest titles to the latest bestsellers. Though this is the original, there are 15 other branches in Dublin, including ones at Nassau Street and Heuston Station. *40 Lower O'Connell St. www.eason.ie.* ☎ *01/858-3800. Map p 78.*

★ Hodges Figgis GRAFTON STREET

Another enormous *grande dame* Dublin bookshop, this one's even older than Eason's—they've been dealing in the printed page here since 1768. Now owned

★★ **Harvey Nichols** DUNDRUM The only Irish outpost of the famous British department store chain, "Harvey Nicks" is as renowned for its outstanding food court as it is for its high-end fashion and beauty. There's also a good steakhouse and trendy cocktail bar. Harvey Nichols is in the Dundrum Town Centre mall, 8km (5 miles) south of Dublin city center. It has late-night shopping until 9pm, Wednesday to Friday. *Dundrum Town Center, Sandyford Rd. www. harveynichols.com.* ☎ *01/291-0488. Map p 78.*

Fashion & Clothing
★ **BT2** GRAFTON STREET A more cutting-edge spin-off of the department store Brown Thomas (see above), BT2 sells youthful designer fashions for men and women. It also has the biggest denim bar in Ireland, full of hip brand names such as Supertrash and 7 For All Mankind. BT2 also has a branch in the **Dundrum Town Centre** mall (☎ 01/296-8400). *28–29 Grafton St. www.bt2.ie.* ☎ *01/605-6747. Map p 77.*

★ **China Blue** TEMPLE BAR Shelves upon shelves of women's and men's footwear can be found at this trendy shoe store—including an enticing range of designer Doc Martens. It also sells a good selection of kids' shoes. *Merchants Arch, Temple Bar. www. chinablueshoes. com.* ☎ *01/671-8785. Map p 78.*

★★★ **Claire Garvey** TEMPLE BAR One of the top young Irish fashion designers to have emerged in the 21st century so far, Claire Garvey sells beautiful, bold, and feminine creations from her boutique on über-trendy Cow's Lane. Her creations are full of elegance and dramatic flair, true one-of-a-kind items. *8 Cow's Lane. www. clairegarvey.com.* ☎ *01/671-7287. Map p 78.*

★ **Costelloe & Costelloe** GRAFTON STREET This sweet clothing and accessories store sells a great range of handbags, pashminas, shrugs, and—delightfully—fascinators and headpieces. Best of all, prices are thoroughly reasonable. *14A Chatham St.* ☎ *01/671-4209. Map p 78.*

★★★ **Design Centre** CITY CENTER Located in the Powerscourt Townhouse Centre (see p 87), this is a great showcase for Irish fashion designers, both new and established. A lot of what's on offer

Window display at Arnotts.

Brown Thomas on Grafton Street.

is unsurprisingly expensive, but you can sometimes walk away with a bargain. *Powerscourt Centre, South William St. www.designcentre.ie.* ☎ *01/679-5863. Map p 78.*

★ **Kevin & Howlin** COLLEGE GREEN There's nothing cutting-edge whatsoever about this place—and that's just why people like it. Dublin's go-to store for Donegal tweed has been selling hand-woven jackets, coats, hats and other traditional Irish countryware since 1936. *31 Nassau St. www.kevinandhowlin.com.* ☎ *01/633-4576. Map p 77.*

★★★ **Louise Kennedy** MERRION SQUARE Undoubtedly one of the biggest names in contemporary Irish fashion—so respected that they put her on a postage stamp a few years ago—Louise Kennedy has dressed everyone from heads of state to Hollywood superstars. Her boutique in Merrion Square showcases the best of her current collection. Among the items she's famous for is the gorgeous "Kennedy bag," a limited-edition handbag that became the must-have accessory among the Irish *glitterati* in 2013— yours for a mere €1,500. *356 Merrion Sq. www.louisekennedy.com.* ☎ *01/662-0056. Map p 78.*

★ **Mad Hatter** CITY CENTER Going for a day at the races? Preparing for that special event? Talented milliner Nessa Cronin sells her quirky, original, elegant, and fun designs here, alongside hats by other top European designers. She also has a range of handbags, jewelry, and other accessories—but the headgear's always the star. *20 Lower Stephen St. www.madhatterhat.com.* ☎ *01/405-4936. Map p 78.*

★★★ **Om Diva** CITY CENTER Proof that not every designer emporium has to be the kind of place where they check your credit rating at the door, Om Diva is a

Grafton Street.

Prime Shopping Zones

Centerpiece to the Southside's shopping experience is the pedestrianized **Grafton Street,** with Brown Thomas, Weir, and a host of reliable fashion chains all heaving at weekends. Running off that is **Johnson's Court** alleyway with diamond jewelry aplenty, leading to the majestic **Powerscourt Townhouse Centre,** which contains an antiques arcade and the Design Centre. Near Trinity College, **Nassau Street** has a good collection of shops for quality crafts and gifts, including Kilkenny and House of Ireland, and **Dawson Street** has bookstores. For antique furniture and jewelry, head to **Francis Street** near St. Patrick's Cathedral. In the southern suburbs, the huge **Dundrum Town Centre** attempts to lure shoppers away from the center, with a vast mall of upmarket high-street names including Harvey Nichols. **Temple Bar** has weekend outdoor markets, quirky clothes, and record stores. North of the Liffey, vast **O'Connell Street** houses the much-loved department store Clery's, plus Eason bookstore and Penney's for cheap fashions.

delightful, cheery place with a great selection of designer women's fashion, handmade jewelry, vintage clothes, and accessories. One of Dublin's real finds. *27 Drury St. www.omdivaboutique.com.* ☎ *01/679-1211. Map p 77.*

Gourmet Food

★★ Butlers Chocolate Café

GRAFTON STREET These chocolatiers now sell their delicious wares all over the world, but the business is still owned and run by the same Dublin family who founded it in 1932. Their Chocolate Cafes are all over Dublin, including Grafton Street, Henry Street, and the airport, but the one on Wicklow Street is the flagship. In addition to an enormous selection of gourmet chocolates, Butlers also sells cakes, cookies, flapjacks—and make a mean cup of joe. The hot chocolate is spectacular; try the white-chocolate version for the purest hit of sweet choccy joy. True addicts can take a tour of the Butlers factory,

just north of Dublin (see p 33). *24 Wicklow St. www.butlerschocolates. com.* ☎ *01/671-0591. Map p 77.*

★★★ Fallon & Byrne CITY

CENTER This exceptional artisan food and wine store is like a high-end deli crossed with an old-fashioned grocer's—albeit a posh, modern version. Produce is laid out in open crates and the shelves are stocked with epicurean treats of all kinds, including cheese, charcuterie, and a great selection of wine. An outstanding **restaurant** (see p 105) is on the top floor. *11–17 Exchequer St. www.fallon andbyrne.com.* ☎ *01/472-1010. Map p 78.*

★★★ Sheridans Cheesemongers GRAFTON STREET Serious

cheese lovers need look no further than this wonderful cheesemonger on South Anne Street. Sheridans stocks around 100 different varieties of cheese—French, English, Italian, you name it—but traditional Irish varieties are its particular specialty.

It also sells other deli items, such as wine and cold meats, and does sandwiches to go. *11 S. Anne St. www.sheridanscheesemongers.com.* ☎ *01/679-3143. Map p 77.*

Household & Gifts

★★★ **Avoca** CITY CENTER A Dublin institution, Avoca is a wonderland of vivid colors, intricately woven fabrics, soft blankets, light woolen sweaters, children's clothes, and toys, all in a delightful shopping environment spread over three floors near Trinity College. All the fabrics are woven in the Vale of Avoca in the Wicklow Mountains. The store also sells pottery, jewelry, vintage and antique clothing, food, and adorable little things you really don't need but can't live without. Hands down, this is one of the best stores in Dublin. The top-floor **cafe** (see p 103) is a great place for lunch. *www.avoca.ie. 11–13 Suffolk St.* ☎ *01/677-4215. Map p 78.*

★★ **The Design Tower** GRAND CANAL QUAY A cutting-edge convocation of hot designers and craftspeople work at this former sugar refinery at the Grand Canal Quay on the eastern side of the city. Occupants include Seamus Gill, who makes extraordinary,

Vintage Market floor of Avoca.

Sheridans Cheesemongers on South Anne Street.

almost organic-seeming silverware; conceptual artist and fashion designer Roisin Gartland; and jewelry designer Brenda Haugh, whose work includes interesting modern interpretations of Celtic motifs. Some designers here have walk-in shops, but most prefer appointments, so call ahead if you want to see someone specific. The Design Tower is near Grand Canal Dock DART station, or about a 20-minute walk from Grafton Street. *Trinity Centre, Pearse St. & Grand Canal Quay. www.thedesigntower.com.* ☎ *01/677-5655. Map p 78.*

★ **House of Ireland** COLLEGE GREEN An excellent "one-stop shop" for quality Irish souvenirs, this is the place to come for Waterford and Galway Crystal, Belleek China, jewelry, linens, and clothing by big-name Irish designers such as Eugene and Anke McKernan, John Rocha, and Louise Kennedy. Just one trip here and nobody back home needs to know that you didn't really scour the country for that perfect knick-knack or gift. If you've left your souvenir shopping until the last minute, two smaller outlet branches are at Dublin Airport. *www.houseof ireland.com. 38 Nassau St.* ☎ *01/671-1111. Map p 77.*

Browsing the colorful designs at the Designer Mart on Cow's Lane.

★★★ **Mayfly** TEMPLE BAR This Temple Bar charmer (look for the cow in the buggy out front) is a treasure trove for deliciously creative, artsy gifts, jewelry, clothing, and other doodads that are impossible to resist. Artists whose work is for sale include Courtney Tyler, who turns old watch faces into interesting jewelry, and James Carroll, a designer of furniture and homeware known for his unusual and playful creations. *11 Fownes St. Upper. www.mayfly.ie.* ☎ *086/376-4189. Map p 78.*

★★★ **Moss Cottage** DUN-DRUM A real one-of-a-kind craft store, Moss Cottage is the kind of

Artist at the KEMP Gallery in the DESIGNyard.

place where you go in for a browse and leave with bags full of souvenirs and a mental note to e-mail the lovely owner pictures of all your finds *in situ* back home. It specializes in "upcycling"—converting old junk into beautiful things—and stocks everything from scented candles to vintage homewares. The shop is in the suburb of Dundrum, about 7km (4½ miles) south of the city center. *4 Pembroke Cottages. www.mosscottage.com.* ☎ *01/215-7696. Map p 78.*

Jewelry

★★★ **DESIGNyard** COLLEGE GREEN Some of Ireland's leading designers of contemporary jewelry have creations for sale here. Prices tend to be quite high—the cheapest items are around €100 and rise to thousands—but you'll be walking away with something beautiful and unique. DESIGNyard has an especially beautiful range of engagement rings. *25 S. Frederick St. www.designyard.ie.* ☎ *01/474-1011. Map p 77.*

★★ **Gollum's Precious** CITY CENTER Come here for classic vintage and designer jewelry—especially French. It also has a particularly good collection of contemporary pearl earrings, bracelets, and necklaces. *Ground Floor, Powerscourt Centre.* ☎ *01/670-5400. Map p 78.*

★ Rhinestones COLLEGE GREEN

This small but delightful jewelry store specializes in costume jewelry, both contemporary and vintage. The antique pieces go back to the early Victorian age, but the mid-20th-century collection has a particular air of glamour. *18 St. Andrew St.* ☎ *01/679-0759. Map p 78.*

★★ Weir & Sons GRAFTON STREET

Established in 1869, this is the granddaddy of Dublin's fine jewelry shops. It sells new and antique jewelry, as well as silver, china, and crystal. The ground floor of the main branch on Grafton Street also has a section devoted to 17th-, 18th-, and 19th-century antique silver from Ireland and Britain. A second branch can be found in Dundrum, about 7km (4⅓ miles) south of the city center. *96–99 Grafton St. www.weirandsons.ie.* ☎ *01/677-9678. Map p 77.*

Markets & Malls

★★ Designer Mart at Cow's Lane TEMPLE BAR

This glamorous showcase for fashion designers and craftspeople from all over Ireland takes place in the über-trendy

Temple Bar Book Market.

Weir & Sons on Grafton Street.

Cow's Lane every Saturday from 10am to 5pm. *Merrion Square. Map p 78.*

★ Dundrum Town Centre DUNDRUM

To the south of the city center, this enormous shopping mall is filled with top-name brands, chain stores, and boutiques—in addition to all the cafes and restaurants you could want to help refuel those shop-weary feet. The mall is right next to the Balally Luas (tram) stop. *Sandyford Rd. www.dundrum.ie.* ☎ *01/299-1700. Map p 78.*

★★ Powerscourt Townhouse Centre CITY CENTER

In a restored 1774 town house, this four-story complex consists of a central sky-lit courtyard and more than 60 boutiques, craft shops, art galleries, snack bars, wine bars, and restaurants. The wares include all kinds of crafts, antiques, paintings, prints, ceramics, leatherwork, jewelry, clothing, chocolates, and farmhouse cheeses. You can also book a behind-the-scenes tour to learn more about the house's history, where you'll poke around the old kitchen and cellars, the former Lord and Lady's bedrooms and dressing rooms, the music room, ballroom, and dining room. For details and

Temple Bar Food Market.

booking, contact Shireen Gail on
☎ **086/806-5505,** or e-mail
shireengail@gmail.com. *59 S. William St. www.powerscourtcentre.
com.* ☎ *01/679-4144. Map p 78.*

★ Temple Bar Book Market

TEMPLE BAR   This pleasant, low-
key market takes up residence in
Temple Bar Square all weekend
from 11am to 6pm; there's always
some piece of printed treasure or
other to be unearthed among its
secondhand book stalls. *Temple Bar
Square. Map p 78.*

★★ Temple Bar Food Market

TEMPLE BAR   A must for foodies,
this market makes its presence felt
more than any other in the city, as
tempting aromas waft around
Meeting House Square from 10am
to 4:30pm every Saturday. Should
the weather take a turn for the
worse, there's even a fancy retract-
able roof to keep you dry while you
deliberate over which Irish farmhouse cheese to take away, before
waiting in line for a freshly cooked
snack. *Meeting House Square,
Temple Bar. Map p 78.*

Music

★★★ Claddagh CITY CENTER

Renowned among insiders in traditional Irish music circles, this is
where to find "the genuine article"
in traditional music and perhaps
discover a new favorite. Not only is
the staff knowledgeable and enthu-
siastic about new artists, but they're
able to tell you which venues and
pubs are hosting the best music
sessions that week. A second
branch is at 2 Cecilia St., Temple
Bar (☎ 01/677-0262). *5 Westmoreland St. http://claddaghrecords.com.*
☎ *01/888-3600. Map p 78.*

★★ Waltons CITY CENTER   A

longtime favorite among Dublin's
musically-inclined (of which you
might have noticed there are
many), Waltons has been in business since the 1920s. They have an
excellent stock of Irish folk instruments, including penny whistles,
flutes, accordions, and pipes, as
well as a huge range of traditional
Irish music CDs, books, and
T-shirts. *69 South Great George's St.
www.waltons.ie.* ☎ *01/475-0661.
Map p 78.* ●

St. Stephen's Green & Iveagh Gardens

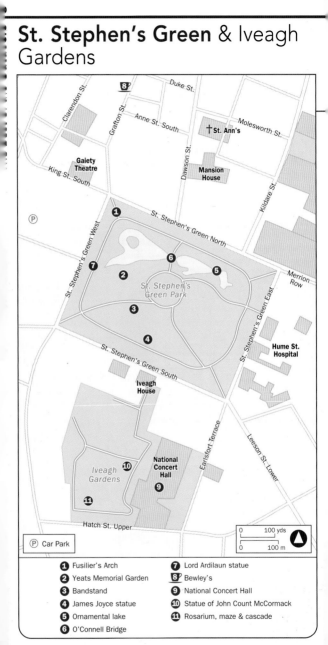

Key

1. Fusilier's Arch
2. Yeats Memorial Garden
3. Bandstand
4. James Joyce statue
5. Ornamental lake
6. O'Connell Bridge
7. Lord Ardilaun statue
8. Bewley's
9. National Concert Hall
10. Statue of John Count McCormack
11. Rosarium, maze & cascade

Previous page: Fusiliers' Arch.

St. Stephen's Green is adored by locals, who flock to its verdant lawns at the first sight of the sun. You can relax here for hours, explore the grounds dotted with sculptures, and enjoy the music and performances. Just a minute's walk away are the tranquil Iveagh Gardens, exquisite in their near desolation. Nearby, yet a world away. START: **Northwest corner of St. Stephen's Green.** ⏱ **2 hr.**

① ★ **Fusiliers' Arch.** The huge Ballyknockan granite arch, nearly 10m (33 ft) high, marks the northwest entrance to St. Stephen's Green. Built in 1907, and a replica of the Arch of Titus in Rome, it's a memorial to young Irish soldiers who died in the Boer War between 1899 and 1900. Stand underneath to read the engraved names of more than 230 who fell in battle. Republicans unofficially renamed it as Traitors' Gate, as this war was seen as a fight between Imperialist and Republican ideals and far from the Irish struggle. Sharp eyes might spy the bullet marks on the northeast face around the words "*Laings Nek*," thought to be from the 1916 Uprising. ⏱ *5 min. Northwest corner of St. Stephen's Green.*

② ★★ **Yeats Memorial Garden.** One of the most beloved monuments in St. Stephen's Green is the bronze sculpture by British artist Henry Moore of William Butler Yeats. Made in 1967, *Knife Edge* portrays the angular looks of the Dublin-born Nobel Prize–winning author and poet, who was a

Pond in St. Stephen's Green.

founder of the Irish Literary Revival of the late 19th century. It stands at the edge of the Yeats Memorial Garden, a small amphitheater with occasional theatrical performances in summer. ⏱ *20 min.*

③ ★ **Bandstand.** As befitting any garden of the era, this typical piece of Victoriana has cast-iron supports and a wooden roof. Built to celebrate Queen Victoria's Jubilee in 1888, it hosts lunchtime concerts on most summer days (check the noticeboard at the northwest entrance for listings) ranging from jazz and folk to swing. Most concerts start around 1pm, so lie back and enjoy. All that's missing is a decent cafe nearby. ⏱ *5 min.*

④ ★ **James Joyce statue.** Near the bandstand, poor old James Joyce makes a meek figure, tiny head mounted on a huge plinth. Now considered to be Ireland's most celebrated writer, it's strange to think that he was rejected by his own people at the time, who considered him to be far too liberal and out of step with the prevailing middle-class, Catholic, conservative

Contrasting Spaces

The 9 hectares (22 acres) of St. Stephen's Green have been a popular public space in the city center ever since 1880 when Lord Ardilaun opened them up—not bad for a former leper colony and public hanging spot. But if St. Stephen's Green is a public park, **Iveagh Gardens** is the secret garden, all statues with missing arms, fountains, wooded walks, and Gothic, ivy-clad corners. Built by Ninian Niven in 1863, this was originally the private gardens of Iveagh House. Many locals say it's the city's best-kept secret. St. Stephen's Green is open Monday to Saturday from 7:30am and on Sundays and public holidays from 9:30am. Closing time at St. Stephen's Green is 20 minutes before darkness; Iveagh Gardens opens half an hour later and closes at 6pm (Mar–Oct); 4pm (Nov and Feb); and 3:30pm (Dec and Jan).

culture of the era. St. Stephen's Green was one of several prominent landmarks that epitomized "dear, dirty Dublin" for him, although he spent most of his life in self-appointed exile. Follow his gaze over the road to Newman House, once the Catholic University where he studied. ⏲ *5 min.*

❺ ★ Ornamental lake. The artificial lake stretches across the northern end of the green, built by Arthur Guinness as part of his landscaping for public enjoyment. The lake, fed by an artificial waterfall near the bridge, is very popular with kids, especially when they get to feed the ducks swimming past. ⏲ *10 min.*

Picnic in St. Stephen's Green.

❻ ★ O'Connell Bridge. No, not the immense multi-lane highway crossing the Liffey but a little stone humpbacked bridge over the lake. It's thought to be the original O'Connell Bridge, designed by J.F. Fuller at the time of the green's redesign and built over the middle of the lake. It wasn't until 1882 that the "other" bridge was renamed from Carlisle to O'Connell, after the lawyer who fought for Catholic rights. ⏲ *5 min.*

❼ ★ Lord Ardilaun statue. It's only fitting that the man who financed and created the green has such an imposing statue. The seated figure of Lord Ardilaun looks towards the Guinness brewery at St. James's Gate. Better known as Arthur Guinness, born in 1840 and great-grandson of the original Arthur Guinness, he was something of a philanthropist, not least for purchasing the green in 1877 and giving it to the capital as a public park. As well as financing all the work, he also secured an Act of Parliament that entrusted the maintenance to the Public Works commissioners. ⏲ *5 min.*

8 ★ **Bewley's.** It's a short walk up Grafton Street from St. Stephen's Green to this most famous of Dublin cafes, a local landmark since 1927. Fun fact: The distinctive, ornate faux-Egyptian facade (framing its never-really-used full name, "Bewley's Oriental Café") owes its existence to the fact that, when the place opened, Europe was in the grip of a craze for all things Ancient Egyptian, following the discovery of Tutankhamen's tomb just 5 years before. *St. Stephen's Green W. $.*

9 ★★ **National Concert Hall.** A pleasant way of walking between Stephen's Green to Iveagh Gardens is via the side of the National Concert Hall (NCH) on Earlsfort Terrace. It was originally built for the Dublin International Exhibition in 1865, lasting 6 months and attracting nearly 1 million visitors. Redeveloped in 1914 by Rudolph Maximilian in a classical style similar to that of Custom House, it was taken over by University College Dublin and has been a concert hall since 1981. Despite impressive events, the venue is remarkably accessible, especially its lunchtime concerts of popular classics. ⏱ *5 min.*

The National Concert Hall by night.

10 ★ **Statue of John Count McCormack.** Aging, unnamed statues dot the gardens, so it's a lovely contrast to see this one of a more recent Dublin-born hero, sculpted by Elizabeth O'Kane. McCormack (1884–1945) was an iconic tenor, hugely successful in America, where he filled Carnegie Hall and New York's Hippodrome an amazing 12 times in one season. Earning a great fortune, he allegedly had a weakness for horses, and spent vast sums in backing that elusive winner. ⏱ *5 min.*

11 ★★ **Rosarium, Maze, & Cascade.** At the gardens' southern edge, near the Hatch Street exit, take a seat in the fragrant, recently rebuilt **Victorian rosarium**—a peaceful place to sit to seek solitude amongst cerise blooms. This was all part of the private grounds of the Earls of Iveagh, including what was the archery ground used for the International Exhibition in 1865. Most of the beauties have been restored over the years since 1955, including the **maze,** with the sundial as centerpiece. A few feet away on the western side, the vast **cascade** provides the most noise you're likely to hear in the gardens; try to get here for noon to see (and hear) it being switched on, when water thunders over the rocks. ⏱ *45 min.*

Phoenix Park

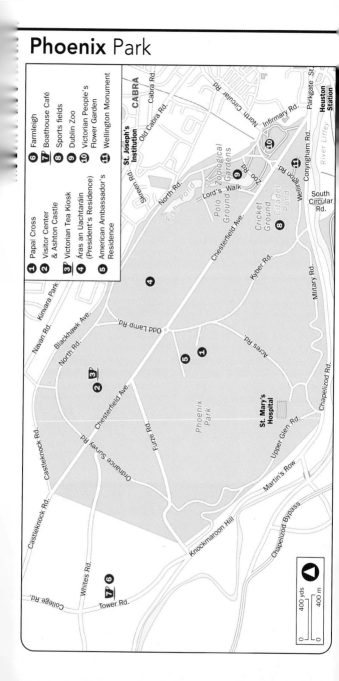

1 Papal Cross
2 Visitor Center & Ashton Castle
3 Victorian Tea Kiosk
4 Áras an Uachtaráin (President's Residence)
5 American Ambassador's Residence
6 Farmleigh
7 Boathouse Café
8 Sports fields
9 Dublin Zoo
10 Victorian People's Flower Garden
11 Wellington Monument

Now considered Dublin's playground, the park was originally built for the rich, with tree-lined avenues, forests, and deer roaming the grasslands. There's no significance to the mythical bird here: The Brits mispronounced its original name *Fionn Uisce* ("clear water") to the more manageable "Phoenix." START: Bus: 25, 51, 68 (Parkgate St.) or 37, 38 (Ashtown Gate). LUAS: Museum. ◷ 2–4 hr.

❶ ★ Papal Cross. The size of this white cross is awesome, stretching to a mammoth 35m (115 ft) high and weighing 40 tons. Startling in its simplicity, this was erected for Pope John Paul II's visit to give Mass on September 29, 1979, to more than 1.25 million people—around one-third of the country's population. The choir alone contained 5,000 people. You can bet that the rest watched it live on TV. These days it's practically deserted, but photos in the **Visitor Centre** show off the Pope's gig in all its glory. Nearby is the area known as **Fifteen Acres**, home to hundreds of deer, descendents of the original residents from Lord Ormonde's day in the 1660s (see ❷).

❷ ★★ Visitor Centre and Ashtown Castle. Phoenix Park was laid out in 1662, initially as a private hunting ground and hawking enclosure for the Duke of Ormonde (1610–1688). Deer still live in the park, albeit safe from both hunters and feckless aristocrats these days. The visitor center does a good job of recounting the history of the park; highlights include an exhibit devoted to the grave of a Viking shield maiden, discovered during building work—although, surprisingly, it's not the best archaeological discovery to have been made here. The visitor center is partly located inside **Ashtown Castle**, a towerhouse built in the 1430s. Amazingly, nobody knew it was even here until 1978, when a later building that had completely engulfed the castle was demolished. Free parking is adjacent to the center. ◷ *30 min.* ☎ *www.phoenixpark.ie. 01/677-0095. Free admission. Apr–Dec daily 10am–6pm; Jan–Mar Wed–Sun 9:30am–5:30pm. Last admission 45 min before closing. Bus: 37.*

❸ ★ Victorian Tea Kiosk. Next to the Visitor Centre, this cute little cafe serves snacks and light lunches and has bathrooms. It's open daily from 10am to 4:30pm. *Visitors' Centre, Phoenix Park, Ashtown Gate* $.

Herd of deer and Papal Cross in Phoenix Park.

④ ★★ Áras an Uachtaráin. This grand 1750s mansion is the official residence of Ireland's head of state (the name literally translates as "the President's House"). It was built as the summer retreat of the Viceroy (governor), whose official residence was at Dublin Castle (see p 40, ③). Every Saturday there are free guided tours of the building—but on a first-come, first-served basis—which allow visitors to see the inside, in surprising detail. Tours leave from the Phoenix Park Visitor Centre every hour from 10:30am. Due to security restrictions, backpacks, large bags, baby strollers, cameras, and mobile phones are all forbidden. ⏱ *1 hr. Dame St. See p 45, ②.*

⑤ American Ambassador's Residence. Built in 1774, this is, unsurprisingly, closed to the public. It's still possible to peek through the huge gates to see the past residence of such luminaries as the Duke of Wellington and Sir Robert Peel. ⏱ *5 min.*

⑥ ★ Farmleigh. Once home to the Guinness family, this 32-hectare (78-acre) opulent estate is now open for free guided tours. Hard to believe that it was originally a small Georgian house, until a succession of well-heeled Guinnesses extended it with a ballroom wing and exotic gardens. Access is by guided tour only; highlights include the hallways festooned with huge portraits, 7.5m- (25 ft) high tapestries, and Venetian chandeliers, replicas of those in London's Houses of Parliament. Incredible that even such a wealthy family often lived in a couple of rooms in winter to save on heating costs. The ⏱ *1 hr. Castleknock, Phoenix Park. www. farmleigh.ie.* ☎ *01/815-5900. Free admission. Mid Mar–late Dec Tues–Sun & bank-holiday Mon 10am–6pm; last admission to grounds 1 hr before closing. Tours approx every hour 10:15am–4:15pm. Bus: 37.*

⑦ ★★ The Boathouse Café. Overlooking the ornamental lake at Farmleigh, this pleasant cafe offers seasonal menus and delicious, healthful snacks. *Farmleigh.* ☎ *01/ 815-7255. Open with house. $.*

⑧ ★ Sports Fields. The park has more than 2,300 sporting fixtures every year, and on summer weekends the sports fields crackle with the energy of cricket, hurling, and

Phoenix Park tea rooms.

The residence of the American Ambassador.

even polo matches. The **All Ireland Polo Club,** founded in 1873 and Europe's oldest polo club, has its home here. Sit back on a sunny Sunday and watch the "King of Games" in all its thunderous glory, albeit amid smaller crowds than a tournament in 1909 that saw 30,000 spectators. The cricket pitch also has a noble history, its earliest recorded match played here in 1792. The **Phoenix Cricket Club,** founded in 1830, has played here from 1853 till today. John Stuart Parnell was one of its founder members, and his son Charles Stewart, famous for bringing Irish home rule to the fore was once their captain. The park is a little different from the days when women were only allowed to watch from their carriages outside—thankfully anyone can take in some hurling or Gaelic football, the occasional cycle race, or even horseracing. ① 10 min., or upwards of 1½ hr. to watch a game. All Ireland Polo Club: www.allirelandpolo club.com. ☎ 087/286-9691. Season: May–Sept, Sat & Sun 3pm (weather permitting). Phoenix Cricket Club: www.phoenixcricketclub.com. ☎ 01/677-0121.

❾ ★★ Dublin Zoo. You might want to peep at some panthers, ogle at the elephants, or gawp at giraffes. The zoo, one of Europe's oldest, has been expanded recently to give the animals more space. Even the monkeys are guaranteed

Dublin Zoo.

Phoenix Park: Practical Matters

Spanning 700 hectares (1,730 acres), twice the size of New York's Central Park, Phoenix Park has two separate entrances, of which Park Gate is easier to access and is right by the bicycle rental. Weekends, especially during summer, have more on offer, including sporting events and tours of **Áras an Uachtaráin** (President's Residence) every Saturday. Officials the park is open 24 hours daily, but late-night walks are not recommended. Information: ☎ 01-677 0095. Entrances on Parkgate St. & Ashtown Gate. Park: www.phoenixpark.ie. Free admission.

to prompt squeals of excitement from the little ones. ⏲ *2 hr.* See p 32, ➐.

➓ ★★ Victorian People's Flower Garden.
Stretching over an area of 9 hectares (22 acres), this is the place for a quiet respite and

Wellington Monument.

peaceful walks. Laid out around 1840 and opened up in 1864 under George William Frederick Howard, 7th Earl of Carlisle, this is typical of gardens of the time, with an attractive horticultural layout, ornamental lakes, and Victorian bedding schemes. ⏲ *1 hr.*

⓫ ★ Wellington Monument.
Visible from afar, Europe's tallest obelisk at 62m (205 ft.) was completed in 1861 to commemorate the victories of Dublin-born Arthur Wellesley, Duke of Wellington. Climb the stone steps at its base to admire the bronze plaques on four sides: cast from cannons captured at Waterloo, three plaques have murals representing Wellington's career, the fourth being an inscription; the *Indian Wars* by Joseph Kirk is particularly worth a look. It's also a lovely spot for catching a few rays of sun with views of the lush lawns below. If you think the monument is impressive, imagine what it would have looked like with the statue of Wellesley on horseback on the top—which was planned, but shortage of funds curtailed that idea. ⏲ *10 min.* ●

6

The Best Dining

Dublin Dining

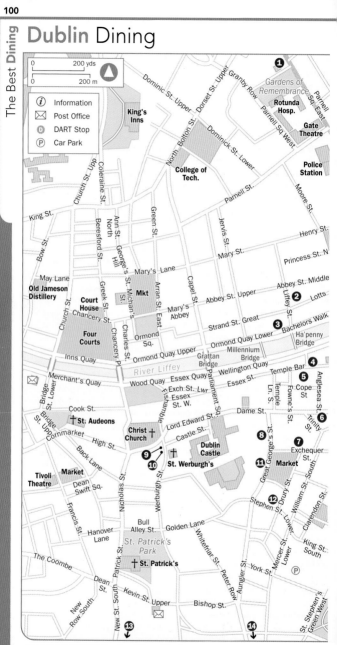

Previous page: Seafood on ice at Super Miss Sue.

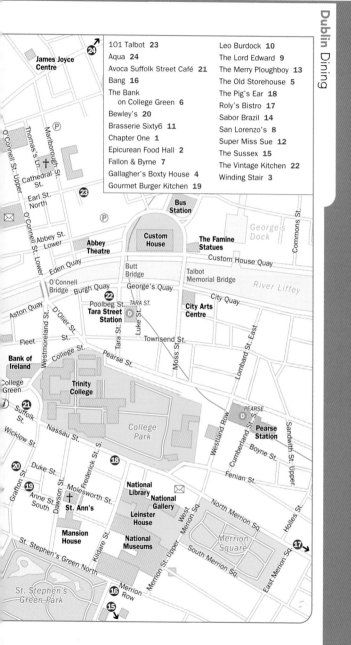

James Joyce Centre 24

101 Talbot 23
Aqua 24
Avoca Suffolk Street Café 21
Bang 16
The Bank
  on College Green 6
Bewley's 20
Brasserie Sixty6 11
Chapter One 1
Epicurean Food Hall 2
Fallon & Byrne 7
Gallagher's Boxty House 4
Gourmet Burger Kitchen 19

Leo Burdock 10
The Lord Edward 9
The Merry Ploughboy 13
The Old Storehouse 5
The Pig's Ear 18
Roly's Bistro 17
Sabor Brazil 14
San Lorenzo's 8
Super Miss Sue 12
The Sussex 15
The Vintage Kitchen 22
Winding Stair 3

Dining Best Bets

Best **Traditional Reinvention**
★★★ Gallagher's Boxty House $$
20–21 Temple Bar (p 106)

Most **Handsome Dining Room**
★★ Bank on College Green $$ 20
College Green (p 104)

Best **Pre-Theater Meal**
★★★ Chapter One $$$$ 18–19
Parnell Sq. (p 104)

Best **Burger**
★★ Gourmet Burger Kitchen $
Temple Bar Sq. (p 106)

Best **In-Store Replenish**
★★ Avoca $ 11–13 Suffolk St.
(p 103)

101 Talbot.

Best for **Fast Food**
★★ Epicurian Food Hall $ Liffey
St. Lower. (p 105)

Most **Wow Factor Breakfast**
★★ San Lorenzo's $$ South Great
George's St. (p 110)

Best **Food Adventure**
★★★ Sabor Brazil $$$ 50 Pleas-
ants St. (p 109)

Best **Wine List**
★★ Winding Stair $$$ 40 Lower
Ormond Quay $$$ (p 112)

Most **Creative Main Courses**
★ The Pig's Ear $$$ Nassau St.
(p 108)

Best **Literary Pedigree**
★★ Bewley's Cafe $ 78–79 Grafton
St. (p 104)

Best **Fish & Chips**
★ Leo Burdock $ 23 Christchurch
Place (p 107)

Best **Gastropub**
★★ The Sussex $$ 9 Sussex Terrace (p 111)

Best for **Sea Views**
★ Aqua $$$$ 1 West Pier, Howth
(p 103)

Dublin Dining A to Z

★★ 101 Talbot O'CONNELL STREET *INTERNATIONAL* This cheery and informal spot, a 3-minute walk from the General Post Office on O'Connell Street, is strong on delicious Irish cuisine with global influences and a healthy twist. The bright, airy dining room is lined with modern art. Specials may include seasonal vegetables with Taleggio cheese gratin, or roast Lough Erne lamb with herb-encrusted potato rosti. The early bird menu (two courses for €20, 5–7:15pm) is a particularly good deal and popular with pre-theater diners attending the Abbey Theatre just around the corner. *101 Talbot St. www.101talbot.ie.* ☎ *01/874-5011. Entrees €16–€24. Lunch & dinner Tues–Sat. Map p 100.*

★★★ Aqua HOWTH *SEAFOOD* With a jaw-dropping view over Dublin Bay, this has to be one of the most romantic dining spots in the region. You can start with a half dozen oysters from Carlingford Lough before moving on to roast cod with a tomato and chorizo sauce, or some roast monkfish with a curry infusion. There's also a small range of tasty meat options for those who aren't wowed by the bounty of the sea. Howth is a small commuter suburb of Dublin, about 16km (10 miles) northeast of the city center. The restaurant is about a 10-minute walk from the Howth DART station. A cab out here from the city should run you about €30. Definitely worth the splurge. *1 West Pier, Howth.* ☎ *01-832 069. www.aqua.ie. Entrees €17–€42. Lunch & dinner Tues–Sun. DART: Howth. Map p 100.*

★★ Avoca Suffolk Street Café CITY CENTER *CAFE* So much better than just another department store cafe, this is a great place for breakfast, lunch, or a mid-shopping snack. Lunches are healthy and delicious—think crab salad with home-baked bread or a plate of Middle Eastern–style mezze made with Wicklow lamb and served with babaghanouj and hummus. The delicious soups are famous among locals. Or you could just drop in for a tempting slice of cake and a restorative cup of tea. *11–13 Suffolk St. www.avoca.ie.* ☎ *01/677-4215. Entrees €3–€12. Breakfast & lunch daily. Map p 100.*

Avoca Suffolk Street Café.

★★ **Bang** ST. STEPHEN'S GREEN *MODERN IRISH* The presence of so many Irish place names on the menu indicates how much this place has embraced the slow-food ethos. The vast majority of ingredients are regionally sourced from specialist Irish producers. You may find Clare Island salmon served with local radishes and pickled cucumber; John Dory from Kilkeel; or perhaps a rib-eye steak from County Fermanagh. Pre-theater set menus cost €25 for two courses. *11 Merrion Row. www.bangrestaurant. com.* ☎ *01/400-4229. Lunch Wed–Sat, dinner Mon–Sat. Map p 100.*

★★ **Bank on College Green** COLLEGE GREEN *PUB* Undoubtedly one of Dublin's most jaw-droppingly handsome interiors, this place would be worth visiting even if it didn't serve great pub food. A small and fairly traditional lunch menu of burgers, fish and chips, sandwiches, and salads gives way to a more extensive selection in the evening, including steaks, pasta, and sharing plates. Come on Sunday for a leisurely brunch or a traditional roast at lunchtime. *20 College Green. www.bankoncollegegreen. com.* ☎ *01/677-0677. Entrees €13–€25. Lunch & dinner daily. Map p 100.*

★★ **Bewley's** GRAFTON STREET *CAFE* A Dublin landmark since 1927, Bewley's has a literary pedigree as well as a historic one. James Joyce was a regular (it makes an appearance in his book *Dubliners*), and a host of subsequent literary greats made this their regular stop-off for a cup of joe and a slice of cake. It's still hugely popular, but not just for coffee; you can get a pretty good pizza, salad, or burger here, in addition to a more modest menu of light snacks. *78–79 Grafton St. www.bewleys. com.* ☎ *01/672-7720. Breakfast* (from 8am), lunch & dinner daily. *Map p 100.*

★★ **Brasserie Sixty6** CITY CENTER *INTERNATIONAL* This cheerful, well-run bistro near Trinity College is a popular choice with locals for special occasions. Roast meats cooked rotisserie style are a specialty. Try the garlic-and-lemon chicken served with herb stuffing and a bunch of sides, or dig into citrus-glazed duck with potatoes roasted in duck fat. The rest of the menu is made up of modern bistro fare such as roast monkfish with artichokes or a simple, juicy steak with fondant potatoes and peppercorn sauce. Vegetarians are catered to as well, with choices such as vegetable tagine and haloumi Caesar salad, and pretty much all of the food is celiac-friendly. A popular brunch IS served until 4pm on Sundays, accompanied by a live jazz band. *66 Great George's St. www. brasseriesixty6.com.* ☎ *01/400-5878. Entrees €12–€33. Lunch & dinner daily. Map p 100.*

★★★ **Chapter One** O'CONNELL STREET *FRENCH* The vaulted basement of the excellent **Dublin Writers Museum** (see p 13, ❶) houses one of the city's most feted restaurants, with a fixed-price menu that makes excellent use of local flavors and organic

Chapter One restaurant.

Waterside dining at Aqua.

ingredients. Feast on gourmet dishes such as seabass, cockles, and mussels with smoked cod roe cream, or duck breast with baked celeriac. The separate set menu for vegetarians has dishes such as aged cauliflower prepared with pine nut and walnut milk. Adventurous diners will relish the chef's table: Seated in a little booth right inside the kitchen, guests are served a special six-course menu (€100 per person) while the culinary theater happens before your eyes. **Tip:** The lunch menu is only half the price of dinner. *18–19 Parnell Sq. www.chapteronerestaurant.com.* ☎ *01/873-2266. Fixed-price menu €40. Lunch Tues–Fri; dinner Tues–Sat. Map p 100.*

★ **Epicurian Food Hall** O'CON-NELL STREET *FOOD HALL* An energetic coming together of flavors from disparate corners of the global village, this delightful food hall is a voyage of discovery for the epicurious. The selection of lunch options changes quite regularly, but long-standing kitchens include **Istanbul,** specializing in Mediterranean dishes and Turkish kebabs; **Saburritos,** which serves a combination of authentic and California-style Mexican street food; **Rafa's Temaki,** which claims to be the first

place in Ireland to sell temaki (a healthful, fast-food-style combination of Japanese sushi and sashimi); and **La Corte**, an Italian deli. The various stalls share a common seating area, or you can order it to go. *1 Liffey St. Lower. www.epicurean foodhall.ie.* ☎ *01/283-6077. Entrees €4–€13. Breakfast (from 9am), lunch & dinner (until 8pm) daily. Map p 100.*

★★ **Fallon & Byrne** CITY CEN-TER *MODERN FRENCH/IRISH* A top-floor adjunct to the wonderful food and wine store **Fallon & Byrne Food Hall** (p 84), this restaurant serves delicious, seasonal Irish fare sourced from artisan producers. Nothing seems to have come very far from the tiny port of Castletownbere, County Cork; lamb from Lough Erne; and oysters from Carlingford. The menu strikes a nice balance between ambitious dishes and more down-to-earth options, so while you may find turbot served with pink grapefruit and crushed new potatoes, you could just as easily opt for a simple burger topped with Cashel blue cheese and smoked bacon. Vegetarian and vegan menus are also available. And if you prefer to fend for yourself, an enormous selection of deli items is downstairs, available

Dining Tips

Don't be surprised if you're not ushered to your table as soon as you arrive at some upscale restaurants. This is not a delaying tactic—many of the better dining rooms carry on the old custom of seating you in a lounge while you sip an aperitif and peruse the menu. Your waiter then comes to discuss the choices and take the order. You are not called to your table until your first course is about to be served. You are not under an obligation to order a cocktail, of course. It's perfectly find to order a soft drink or just a glass of water.

to go. *11–17 Exchequer St. www. fallonandbyrne.com.* ☎ *01/472-1010. Entrees €12–€33. Lunch & dinner daily. Map p 100.*

★★★ Gallagher's Boxty House TEMPLE BAR/TRINITY COLLEGE *IRISH* Few restaurants come with a greater appreciation for culinary heritage than this one. "Boxty"—a distinctive kind of potato pancake—is the house signature dish here, served with a variety of delicious meat and fish fillings. Also on the menu are steaks, seafood, and Irish stews. Gallagher's tasty Irish variant on the hamburger is made with cumin-and-garlic-spiced lamb and

caramelized onion. Reservations are recommended on weekends, but even on busy nights they can usually squeeze you in (*squeeze* being the operative word if you're seated in the very cozy basement). *20–21 Temple Bar. www.boxtyhouse.ie.* ☎ *01/677-2762. Entrees €15–€25. Lunch & dinner daily. Map p 100.*

★★ Gourmet Burger Kitchen TEMPLE BAR *BURGERS* This upscale mini-chain makes some of the most reliably good burgers in town. Portions aren't huge but there's something for everyone—get yours classic and simple, or opt for one of the more imaginative creations (such as the Kiwiburger,

Bang restaurant.

Brasserie Sixty6.

served with beetroot and pineapple, or the spicy Habanero, with a fruity chile-tomato salsa). There are plenty of chicken options, salads, and even some good veggie choices, such as the delicious Kumara burger, made with fluffy sweet potato. Dessert options are a little disappointing, but the enormous malted shakes more than make up for that. There's a second Dublin branch at 5 South Anne St. *Temple Bar Square. www.gbk.ie.* ☎ *01/670-8343. Entrees €8–€13. Lunch & dinner daily. Map p 100.*

★ **Leo Burdock** CITY CENTER *FISH & CHIPS* It's virtually de rigueur for passing celebrities to pop in here; the photographic "wall of fame" includes Sandra Bullock, Russell Crowe, and Tom Cruise. But don't come expecting cutting-edge cuisine, because Leo Burdock still trades on the same simple, winning formula it has had since 1913: battered fresh fish (cod, sole, ray, or scampi) and thick chips (like very fat steak fries), all cooked the old-fashioned way, in beef drippings. There are other options on the menu, including hamburgers, but frankly, what's the point of coming to a place like this if you don't order the one thing for which it's world

famous? *2 Werburgh St. www. leoburdock.ie.* ☎ *01/454-0306. Entrees €3–€8. Lunch & dinner daily. Map p 100.*

★ **The Lord Edward** CITY CENTER *SEAFOOD* This super-traditional restaurant above an equally old-fashioned pub has been a city staple since 1890. It almost seems that the menu hasn't changed since 1890 either—but the unreconstructed atmosphere is central to the appeal. Prawns, sole, scallops, lobster, and various other fruits of the sea are served every traditional way you can think of and a few you probably can't. Fans of the Lord Edward love it for the sense of continuity and old-school charm. *23 Christchurch Place. www.lordedward. ie.* ☎ *01/454-2420. Entrees €18– €39. Lunch Wed—Fri, lunch & dinner Wed—Sat. Map p 100.*

★ **The Merry Ploughboy** RATHFARNHAM *IRISH/PUB* An exuberant live show of traditional music and dancing accompanies dinner at this hugely popular pub in Rathfarnham, one of Dublin's farther-flung southern suburbs. Admittedly, it's all very touristy, but you certainly get your money's worth—the show runs for 2 hours, and the food, while limited, is actually pretty good. Expect plates along the lines of beef braised in Guinness served with root vegetables and rosemary jus, or trout in a dill-and-lemon crust. The only real drawback is the time it takes to get here (Rathfarnham is about 6km/3¾ miles from the city center), although a dedicated minibus will pick you up and take you back at the end of the night for the bargain price of €7.50 round-trip. *Edmondstown Rd., Rockbrook, Rathfarnham. www.mpbpub.com.* ☎ *01/493-1495. Entrees €9–€24. Dinner & show €50. Lunch & dinner daily. Map p 100.*

★★ The Old Storehouse

TEMPLE BAR/TRINITY COLLEGE *IRISH/PUB* Delicious, traditional pub food is the order of the day here, with just a hint of bistro style around the edges. Choose from fat, juicy burgers served with vine tomatoes and cocktail sauce; bangers and mash (sausages and mashed potato) with ale gravy; or perhaps some steamed mussels with garlic bread. There's a small wine list, but the beer selection is better. *Crown Alley. www.theold storehouse.ie.* ☎ *01/607-4003. Entrees €13–€20. Lunch & dinner daily. Map p 100.*

★★★ The Pig's Ear COLLEGE

GREEN *MODERN IRISH* A wonderfully inventive approach to traditional Irish tastes pervades at this super-cool restaurant overlooking Trinity College. However, this isn't one of those trendy eateries where the menu is too concerned with being clever to be satisfying. Classic ingredients are imbued with modern flair, as in smoked salmon cured with Earl Grey tea, or roast chicken served with hay-smoked butter, hazelnuts, and kale. You certainly won't be able to miss this place from the outside—just look for the shocking-pink door with a candy-striped awning. *4 Nassau St. www.thepigsear.ie.* ☎ *01/670-3865. Entrees €19–€28. Lunch & dinner Mon--Sat. Map p 100.*

★★ Roly's Bistro BALLSBRIDGE

BISTRO This lovely, easygoing bistro, just down the street from the U.S. Embassy, is one of the best places to eat south of the city center. Local meats and fish predominate; start with some Thai-style Castletownbere crab, or perhaps a traditional leek and potato soup (great comfort food for a cold evening). For the main event, try the roast chicken with colcannon

Gallagher's Boxty House.

Dublin's Dining Scene

Dublin's economic boom years in the early 2000s brought with it a new generation of international, sophisticated restaurants. Ireland embraced foodie culture in a way that it never really had before. As the economy crashed, however, Dublin saw a minor resurgence in the popularity of traditional Irish fare, even in expensive restaurants. That's not to say that the food in Dublin is on the downswing—far from it—it's just become easier to find traditional-style Irish food in the city than it was a decade ago, as Ireland re-embraces and re-invents its national food heritage. Still, Dublin remains a notoriously expensive city in which to eat out. Prices have certainly come down in recent years, but you're likely to pay much more for a meal here than in a comparable U.S. city—maybe about the same as you'd expect to pay in Paris or London. But when the food here is good, it's very good. If you can afford to splurge once or twice while you're in town, you're in for a treat.

potato, or, if you want to splurge a bit, the specialty beef rib-eye, aged for 30 days in 12 feet of Himalayan rock salt. An adjacent café has a slightly more stripped-down fixed-price menu (€22 for 2 courses, or €25 for 3). Reservations are recommended. *7 Ballsbridge Terrace. www.rolysbistro.ie.* ☎ *01/832-0690. Entrees €20–€34. Lunch & dinner daily. Map p 100.*

★★★ **Sabor Brazil** IVEACH GARDENS *BRAZILIAN* A good Brazilian restaurant isn't high on the list of things one expects to find in Dublin—and yet Sabor Brazil not only serves outstanding food, it also delivers a fun and memorable experience. The menu (€100 per person for seven courses; no a la carte) fuses contemporary Brazilian flavors with an Irish inflection: Grilled prawns come with chile and *vatapá* (a Brazilian paste made with tomatoes, peppers, nuts, and coconut milk), and *pastel* (kind of like South American dim sum) is filled with whatever the chef decides is best that day. A

Coco-pops French toast at San Lorenzo's.

vegetarian alternative is always available. Reservations are essential, preferably awhile in advance (with a €25 booking deposit, credited to your check on the night), and the restaurant caters to couples only. *50 Pleasants St., off Camden St. http://saborbrazil.ie.* ☎ *01/475-0304. Tasting menu only €100. Dinner Tues–Sun. Map p 100.*

Lamb chops at the Vintage Kitchen.

★★ **San Lorenzo's** CITY CEN-TER *BREAKFAST/ ITALIAN* This funky Italian restaurant serves good, all-round Italian specials in the evening, but that's not what it's famous for in Dublin. San Lorenzo's is one of the most popular spots in town for brunch at weekends. Abandon your hotel "full Irish" and come here for the heavenly French toast, made with caramelized bananas and topped with a coco-pop square (a kind of breakfast cereal made with chocolate-fla-vored puffed rice), whipped cream, and thick chocolate sauce; or opt for the Belgian waffles with salted caramel ice cream. There's a Latin edge to many of the savory options—*huevos rancheros,* brunch tacos, even a pulled-pork hash. Just be prepared to wait for a table. *S. Great George's St. www.sanlorenzos. ie.* ☎ *01/478-9383. Brunch €9–€19; entrees €7–€38. Lunch & dinner Tues–Fri, Sun; dinner Sat. Map p 100.*

★★ **Super Miss Sue** CITY CEN-TER *SEAFOOD* There are actually three restaurants here under the Super Miss Sue umbrella, each serving up excellent seafood to a trendy crowd. **Luna** is the most for-mal of the three, but the quirky **Café** has the best atmosphere. Cod, tuna, salmon, prawns, and oysters are offered several ways, or you could go for one of the enor-mous house special platters. There are also steaks if the fruits of the sea don't tempt you. Super Miss Sue also does a popular brunch at weekends. Dubliners may tell you that the best of the SMS treats are to be had at the third option— **Cervi,** the excellent "chipper." On Friday nights Cervi does delicious fish, chips, and a soda to go for just €10. *2–3 Drury St. www.supermiss sue.com.* ☎ *01-679 9009. Entrees*

Fresh seafood at Super Miss Sue.

Live music at the Merry Ploughboy pub.

€12–€26. Lunch & dinner daily. Map p 100.

★★ The Sussex FITZWILLIAM SQUARE PUB
One of Dublin's best proponents of gastropub cuisine—the reinvention of traditional Irish cooking into something chic and fashionable—is this refined pub (above another popular bar) 10 minutes' walk south of St. Stephen's Green. The menu takes classic pub fare and prepares it beautifully: fish and chips with pea and mint puree; linguine served with tiger prawns, clams, garlic, and chile; or a delicious house burger served with Cork cheddar. For dessert try the posset (a syllabub-like concoction containing cream and lemon) served with spiced shortbread. *Tip:* The lunch menu is an edited version of what's for dinner—but significantly cheaper. *9 Sussex Terrace. www.thesussex.ie.* ☎ *01/676-2851. Entrees €15–€31. Lunch & dinner daily. Map p 100.*

★★★ The Vintage Kitchen
TARA STREET IRISH An antidote to over-fussy fine dining, the Vintage Kitchen is a stripped-down, funky little restaurant. There aren't many tables, and they don't even have an alcohol license—you're encouraged to bring your own bottle if you want wine. However, the classic Irish cooking is truly excellent, artfully presented in a contemporary style, and generously proportioned as well. Start with Donegal smoked haddock chowder before tackling an enormous chicken supreme with burnt honey and bacon, or a flavorsome dish of

The Winding Stair restaurant and bookstore on Ormond Quay.

cod with Roaring Bay mussels and lumpfish caviar. If dinner here is a bit steep for you, come for lunch— main courses are just €12, and small plates half that. Make reservations for dinner. *7 Poolbeg St. www. thevintagekitchen.ie.* 01/679-8705. *Fixed-price menus €28–€34. Lunch & dinner Tues–Fri, dinner Sat. Map p 100.*

★★ The Winding Stair

ORMOND QUAY *MODERN IRISH* A sweet old bookstore downstairs and a chic restaurant upstairs, Winding Stair is situated a stone's throw from the Ha'penny Bridge. The views of the Liffey are romantic, but it's the inventive modern Irish cooking that pulls in the crowds. After a starter of Dingle Bay crab or spiced beef carpaccio with goat's cheese, you could opt for steamed cockles and mussels with brown shrimp mayo or the beef ribeye with sticky onions. The

Chef Dave Coffey of the Sussex.

enormous wine list, which is helpfully arranged by character rather than region, features several decently priced options. *40 Lower Ormond Quay. http://winding-stair. com.* 01/872-7320. *Entrees €23–€28. Lunch & dinner Mon–Fri, dinner Sat–Sun. Map p 100.* ●

Dublin Nightlife

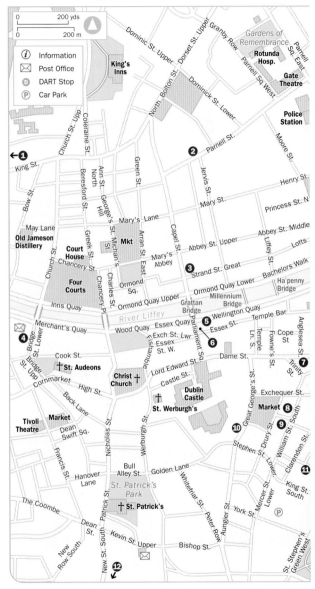

Previous page: The streets of Temple Bar.

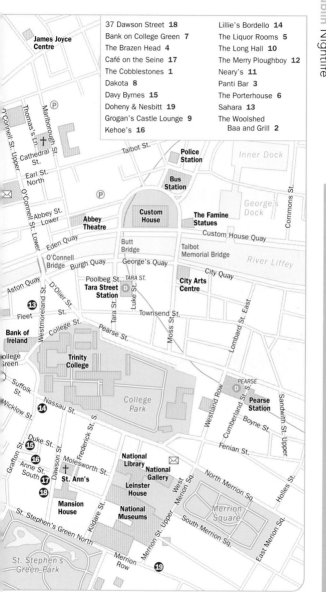

37 Dawson Street **18**	Lillie's Bordello **14**
Bank on College Green **7**	The Liquor Rooms **5**
The Brazen Head **4**	The Long Hall **10**
Café on the Seine **17**	The Merry Ploughboy **12**
The Cobblestones **1**	Neary's **11**
Dakota **8**	Panti Bar **3**
Davy Byrnes **15**	The Porterhouse **6**
Doheny & Nesbitt **19**	Sahara **13**
Grogan's Castle Lounge **9**	The Woolshed
Kehoe's **16**	Baa and Grill **2**

Nightlife Best Bets

Most Jazz Age Throwback
★★★ Café en Seine, *39 Dawson St. (p 117)*

Most Snazzy Cocktails
★★★ The Liquor Rooms, *5 Wellington Quay (p 121)*

Best Literary Credentials
★★ Davy Byrnes, *21 Duke St. (p 118)*

37 Dawson Street Bar.

Best Old World Comfort
★★★ Brazen Head, *20 Lower Bridge St. (p 117)*

Best for Celeb Spotting
★ Lillie's Bordello, *2 Adam Ct., Grafton St. (p 121)*

Best Traditional Music Sessions
★★★ The Cobblestones, *77 N. King St. (p 118)*

Best Artwork
Grogan's Castle Lounge, *15 S. William St. (p 119)*

Best Camp Sunday Night
★★ Panti Bar, *7–8 Capel St. (p 122)*

Best Non-Guinness Stout
★★ Porterhouse, *16–18 Parliament St. (p 121)*

Best Snug
★★ Kehoe's, *9 S. St. Anne St. (p 119)*

Best Chance of Political Intrigue
★★★ Doheny & Nesbitt, *5 Baggot St. Lower (p 118)*

Most Satisfyingly Irish of Irish Pubs
★★★ The Long Hall, *31 S. St. Anne St. (p 120)*

Dublin Nightlife A to Z

Bars & Pubs

★★ 37 Dawson Street ST. STE-PHEN'S GREEN   This sumptuous cocktail bar is crammed with antiques and curios—everything from a stuffed bull's head on a polished wood wall to old anatomical drawings and ornate vases. The cocktail list is as extensive and imaginative as the quirky surroundings would suggest, and at the back of the building is a proper, old-style whiskey bar. It also has a good restaurant. *37 Dawson St.* ☎ *01/902-2908. http://37dawson street.ie. Map p 114.*

★★ Bank on College Green COLLEGE GREEN   This handsome place was built as a bank in 1892, at the height of Victorian opulence. While it's also an appealing place to eat (see p 104), you can enjoy its stunning interior just as well by simply grabbing a pint or a wee dram. *20 College Green. www.bankoncol-legegreen.com.* ☎ *01/677-0677. Map p 114.*

★★★ The Brazen Head USHER'S QUAY   This is a serious contender for the coveted title of "oldest pub in Ireland," having served the locals continually since at least 1661 (although an alehouse was reputedly on the same spot for hundreds of years before that— they claim 1198 as the foundation date, and who's to argue?). It was once a hangout for Irish revolutionaries, and Joyce mentioned the place in *Ulysses,* although today it's more famous for lively traditional music sessions. Every night features a different act; worthies who've played here include Van Morrison, Tom Jones, and Garth Brooks. *20 Lower Bridge St. www.brazenhead. com.* ☎ *01/677-9549. Map p 114.*

★★★ Café en Seine ST. STE-PHEN'S GREEN   At this elegant, 1920s-style cafe/bar, the interior is all terribly Gatsby, with hanging lamps, glass ceilings, faux-baroque furniture, and polished brass statu-ettes. The cocktail list is straight-up fun, the whiskey menu a page long, and the atmosphere appro-priately decadent. A bistro menu is served until 9pm, and on Sundays there's a popular jazz brunch from noon to 5pm. *39 Dawson St. www. cafeenseine.com.* ☎ *01/677-4567. Map p 114.*

Dublin's oldest pub, the Brazen Head.

The Bank on College Green.

★★★ The Cobblestones

SMITHFIELD We recently asked a Dublin taxi driver to recommend the best place for live music in Temple Bar. Answer: "Now why would you bother, when the Cobblestones is so close?" This is an authentic musician's place, as much a traditional music venue as a pub, such is the standard of the music. Free sessions are in the front bar nightly, with ticketed acts in the **Backroom,** a dedicated performance space. *77 N. King St. www. cobblestonepub.ie.* ☎ *01/872-1799. Map p 114.*

★★ Dakota CITY CENTER Small

but perfectly curated, this stylish

Café en Seine.

bar on South William Street has a hip clientele and an outstanding selection of bottled beers and cocktails. The crowd is young and the atmosphere raucously sophisticated. *9 S. William St. www.dakota bar.ie.* ☎ *01/672-7969. Map p 114.*

★★ Davy Byrnes GRAFTON

STREET "He entered Davy Byrnes," wrote Joyce of Leopold Bloom, the hero of *Ulysses.* "Moral pub. He doesn't chat. Stands a drink now and then. But in a leap year once in four. Cashed a cheque for me once." Given the impeccable literary connections of this pub, it's no surprise that so many writers make a pilgrimage to this spot when they're in town. Joyce himself was a regular, although the food has improved since his day—the menu of pub classics and sandwiches is actually pretty good, and reasonably priced. *Ulysses* fans will be delighted to hear that you can still order a gorgonzola sandwich, Bloom's snack of choice. *21 Duke St. www.davybyrnes.com.* ☎ *01/677-5217. Map p 114.*

★★★ Doheny & Nesbitt ST.

STEPHEN'S GREEN From the outside, this pub brings to mind a Victorian medicine cabinet, all polished wood with a rich

Listen to the Music

When you're out for a night of traditional Irish folk music, you should know that some pubs charge and some do not; if the band is playing informally in the main bar, as often happens, there's no charge, although they will probably pass a hat at some point, and everybody should toss in a few euro. If there is a charge, the music usually happens in a separate room from the main pub, and the charge will be noted on the door; usually it's about €5 to €10, and you pay as you go in, cash only. And if they're selling CDs, they'll make sure you know about it. (They'll probably autograph them too, after the set.)

blue-and-gold sign. Its proximity to the political heart of the capital makes it a perennial hangout for politicos, lawyers, economists, and those who write about them—which can make for some spectacularly good eavesdropping. (Its name inspired a catchphrase, "the Doheny & Nesbitt School of Economics," to describe the movers and shakers who used to shoot the breeze here during Ireland's boom years of the 1990s and 2000s.) To admire its cozy interior, a midweek daytime visit is best—this place gets packed in the evenings, especially on summer weekends, and even more so when a big sports match is on. *5 Baggot St. Lower. www.dohenyandnesbitts.ie.* ☎ *01/676-2945. Map p 114.*

★★★ **Grogan's Castle Lounge** CITY CENTER There's a friendly, chatty vibe at this satisfyingly old-fashioned place, considered one of Dublin's "quintessential" pubs. There's nothing modern about the dimly lit, atmospheric interior, save for the incongruous art collection on the walls (ask if you like a piece—most of it is for sale). Grogan's reputation rests mostly on its eclectic clientele, ranging from grizzled old folks who've been coming here for years to hipsterish, artsy types in search of a low-fi hangout. *18 S. William St. www.groganspub.ie.* ☎ *01/677-9320. Map p 114.*

★★ **Kehoe's** GRAFTON STREET This lovely old pub is virtually sepia-toned, with its burnt-orange walls

Enjoy traditional folk music in one of Dublin's pubs.

A traditional Irish music session at Doheny & Nesbitt pub.

and acres of polished walnut. That's an appropriate analogy for the atmosphere too—easy-going and frequently packed in the evenings. Kehoe's is best enjoyed in daylight hours, when you can observe the local characters and soak up the old-school Irish pub atmosphere. A particularly appealing feature are the original "snugs"—tiny private rooms, almost like booths. *9 S. Anne St.* ☎ *01/677-8312. Map p 114.*

★★★ The Long Hall GRAFTON
STREET   The gorgeous, polished walnut-and-brass interior of this Victorian pub is liable to elicit purrs of

Music at the Cobblestones.

delight from thirsty patrons as soon as they walk in the door. Undoubt-edly one of Dublin's most . . . well, *Irish* of pubs, the Long Hall is named for the bar that runs the entire length of the interior. Regu-lars have to fight for space along-side the tourist crowd, but it's more than worth squeezing in for a look at the interior. Not that staying here for a few pints is anything like a chore. *51 S. Anne St.* ☎ *01/677-8312. Map p 114.*

★ The Merry Ploughboy RATH-
FARNHAM   In many ways this is the antithesis to The Cobblestones (see p 118), in that its live music show is very much for tourists—cheesy, but good fun and hugely popular. They will even ferry you here from the city center and take you back again for just €7.50 round-trip. *Edmonstown Rd., Rockbrook, Rathfarnham. www.mpbpub.com.* ☎ *01/493-1495. Map p 114. See also p. 107.*

★ Neary's CITY CENTER   A
favorite hangout of Dublin's the-atergoers—and actors, stage crews, and just about everyone else from the **Gaiety Theatre** (p 134) next door—it's full of Victorian features, such as the wonderful globe

lanterns out front, held aloft by a brass arm emerging from the brickwork. The upstairs bar can be a quiet retreat during the day. *1 Chatham St.* ☎ *01/677-8596. Map p 114.*

★★ The Porterhouse TEMPLE

BAR This lovely pub in Temple Bar was the first in Dublin to sell only microbrewery beers. Most are produced by the Porterhouse's own mini-chain, and the range is constantly updated, so you never know what you'll get from one visit to the next. A relaxed, jovial vibe and hearty pub lunches make it a perfect pit stop on a long day's sightseeing. The pub also does live music every night. *16–18 Parliament St. www.porterhousebrewco.com.* ☎ *01/679-8847. Map p 114.*

★ The Woolshed Baa and Grill

O'CONNELL STREET Looking for somewhere to watch a big game? This is the place. Enormous TV screens flank the bar, showing whatever's hot in the sporting world—football (the European kind), rugby, U.S. sports (including football, the American kind), and whatever else is on the schedule. They also serve crowd-pleasing bar food. *Parnell St. www.woolshedbaa. com.* ☎ *01/872-4325. Map p 114.*

Performers at the Merry Ploughboy.

Nightclubs

★ Lillie's Bordello GRAFTON

STREET One of Dublin's real "VIP" clubs, this long-time celebrity magnet has a notoriously snooty door policy and plenty of roped-off areas to make you feel excluded from the real fun. Still, if glamour is your thing, put on your glitziest gear and act like you just *belong* inside. *2 Adam Ct., Grafton St. www. lilliesbordello.ie.* ☎ *01/679-9204. Daily 11pm–3am. Map p 114.*

★★★ The Liquor Rooms

TEMPLE BAR There's a feel of the speakeasy about this labyrinthine

Kehoe's.

Dublin Nightclubs

Admission to nightclubs varies from free if you arrive early-ish to around €20 for the very fanciest places. Prices are usually higher on Friday and Saturday nights. Check club websites before going so you won't be surprised.

basement club beneath the **Clarence Hotel** (p 142). There are actually two bars down here, with artfully draped doorways and subtle mood lighting that make it easy to get lost and end up in the other bar. The cocktails are outstanding—watching the nimble bartenders at work serves as a reminder that mixology is as much an art as anything. Check out the lively dance floor, or grab a table in one of the many side rooms and watch the time melt away. Reservations are a good idea on weekends. *5 Wellington Quay. www.pod.ie.* ☎ *087/339-3688. Sun–Thurs 5pm–2:30am; Fri–Sat 5pm–4:30am. Map p 114.*

★★ Panti Bar NORTHSIDE One of Dublin's most famous gay clubs—its full name is "Pantibar Homo Activity Centre"—Panti Bar is hugely popular and riotously good fun. Saturday night is cabaret night, often hosted by drag queen Panti Bliss herself, and there's a "gay ole' tea dance" from 3pm on Sundays. Panti's relentless campaigning for gay rights has recently made her quite a public figure; to watch her here, in her natural habitat, in full fabulous flow, is a thing to behold. *7–8 Capel St. www.panti bar.com.* ☎ *01/874-0710. Mon, Wed & Sun 5–11:30pm; Tues 5pm–2am; Thurs–Sat 5pm–2:30am. Map p 114.*

★★ Sahara TEMPLE BAR This cool Temple Bar nightclub has a dash of celebrity cred to go along with its Near Eastern theme (try the delicious, Moroccan-style twist on a Long Island Iced Tea). The latest sounds are on the turntables, the clientele is young, and the atmosphere is suitably laid-back. *10 Westmoreland St. www.saharadublin. com.* ☎ *01/670-8128. Fri–Sat 11pm–3am. Map p 114.*

The bar at Lillie's Bordello.

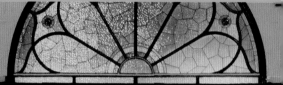

8 The Best Arts & Entertainment

Arts & Entertainment Best Bets

The audience at a concert in the National Concert Hall. Previous page: The Olympia Theatre.

Best **Theater for Kids**
★★ Lambert Puppet Theatre, *Clifton Lane, Monkstown (p 128)*

Best for **Cutting-Edge Opera**
★★ Opera Theatre Company, *various venues, citywide (p 128)*

Best **Sporting Crowds**
★★★ Croke Park, *Jones's Rd.* *(p 131)*, and ★★ Aviva Stadium, *62 Lansdowne Rd. (p 131)*

Best for **Cinephiles**
★★ Irish Film Institute, *6 Eustace St. (p 129)*

Best for **Belly Laughs**
★★ The Comedy Cellar, *21 Wicklow St. (p 128)*

Best for **Beckett Plays**
★★ Gate Theatre, *1 Cavendish Row (p 134)*

Best **Concert Acoustics**
★★ National Concert Hall, *Earlsfort Terrace (p 128)*

Most **Dramatic Architecture**
★★ Grand Canal Theatre, *Grand Canal Sq. (p 176)*

Best for **Blockbuster Gigs**
★ 3Arena, *N. Wall Quay (p 130)*

Best **Daytime Drama**
★★ Bewley's Cafe Theatre, *78–79 Grafton St. (p 134)*

Best **Spun Yarn**
★★★ An Evening of Food, Folklore and Fairies, *20 Lower Bridge St. (p 133)*

Best for **Young Local Bands**
★★ Whelan's, *25 Wexford St. (p 130)*

Best **Family Christmas Show**
★ Gaiety Theatre, *S. King St. (p 134)*

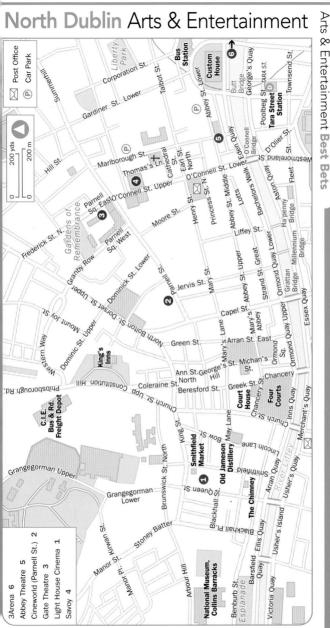

- Post Office
- (P) Car Park

3Arena 6
Abbey Theatre 5
Cineworld (Parnell St.) 2
Gate Theatre 3
Light House Cinema 1
Savoy 4

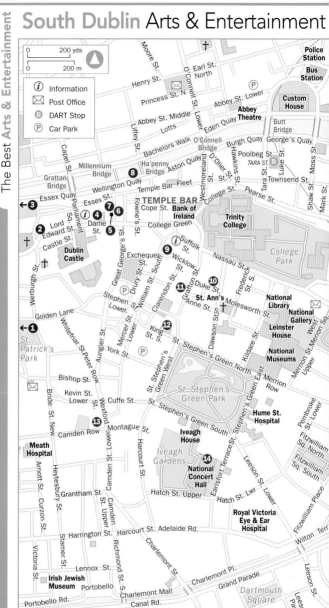

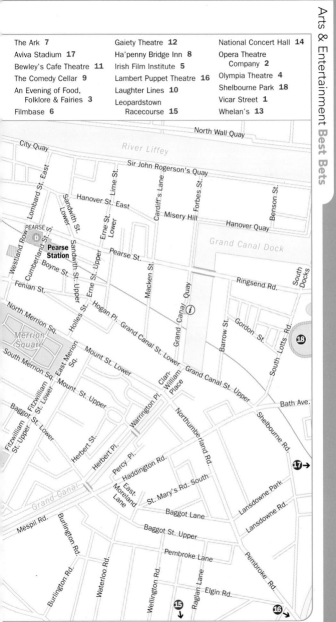

Arts & Entertainment A to Z

Children's Entertainment

★★ Ark TEMPLE BAR The wonderful cultural center is aimed specifically at arts, exhibitions, and activities for children. Performers from all over the world come here. Summertime is particularly busy; check the website for the full events schedule. *11A Eustace St., Temple Bar. www.ark.ie. ☎ 01/670-7788. Tickets free–€10. Map p 126.*

★★ Lambert Puppet Theatre MONKSTOWN This unique theater puts on productions of classic fairy tales using beautifully crafted puppets. Younger children will love it. *Clifton Lane, Monkstown. www. lambertpuppettheatre.com. ☎ 01/280-0974. Tickets €11–€13. DART: Salthill & Monkstown. Map p 126.*

Classical Music & Opera

★★ National Concert Hall IVEACH GARDENS One of the premier venues in Ireland for classical music, this is the permanent home of the RTÉ National Symphony Orchestra. The program also covers opera, world music, jazz, show tunes, and musicals.

The production of Ariodante at the Opera Theatre Company.

Something is on virtually every night; check the website for full listings. Tickets generally cost between €10 and €20, although big-name concerts are more. Some events are free. *Earlsfort Terrace. www.nch.ie. ☎ 01/417-0000. Map p 126.*

★★ Opera Theatre Company TEMPLE BAR This is the main touring opera company in Ireland, known for innovative, accessible productions of classic and new works. Productions are imaginatively staged; recent examples include Rigoletto reimagined in the world of professional wrestling. Venues change with the show, with prices varying accordingly. *Office: Temple Bar Music Centre, Curved St. www.opera.ie. ☎ 01/679-4962. Map p 126.*

Comedy Clubs

★★ The Comedy Cellar CITY CENTER One of the country's top comedy clubs, the Comedy Cellar showcases the best young contenders in the world of Irish standup one night a week, on Wednesday night, when it takes over the upstairs room of the International Bar on Wicklow Street. Tickets cost €10. *The International, 21 Wicklow St. www.dublincomedycellar.com. ☎ 01/677-9250. Map p 126.*

★ Ha'penny Bridge Inn TEMPLE BAR There's shenanigans every night at this popular bar near the Ha'Penny Bridge in Temple Bar. The most infamous of the regular events is the **Battle of the Axe**— open mic night every Tuesday, where those brave or stupid enough to try their hand in front of the lively audience are ritually slaughtered. Thursdays feature

Cineworld.

headline acts. Check the website for full listings. Admission costs €7. *42 Wellington Quay. http://battleof theaxe.com. ☎ 086/815-6987. Doors open 9pm; show 9:30pm. Map p 126.*

★★ **Laughter Lines** GRAFTON STREET   What is it about Dublin on a Wednesday that everybody needs cheering up? Another mid-week pub takeover, this one happens at the Duke on Duke Street, every Wednesday night at 9pm (show starts 9:30pm). The talented company improvises sketches according to whatever the audience suggests. It's chaotic and great fun. Tickets are €5. *The Duke, Duke St. www.laughterlinesdublin-com.webs. com. ☎ 01/679-9553. Map p 126.*

Movies

★ **Cineworld** NORTHSIDE   The biggest cinema in Ireland, this giant multiplex has 17 screens, with all the bang-up-to-date technology you could wish for (Imax! 3D! D-Box! The power to block mobile phone signals! OK, we lied about the last one). This is the place to come for the latest blockbuster releases. Tickets range from about €9 to €20. *Parnell St. www.cineworld. ie. ☎ 1520/880-444. Map p 125.*

★ **Filmbase** TEMPLE BAR   The stripped-down, artsy cousin to the **Irish Film Institute** (see below), Filmbase has a free exhibition space on its ground floor, usually featuring a free show from local contemporary artists. Filmbase also runs special cinema-related events all year, including talks and screenings. Each November it hosts the excellent **Dublin Web Fest** (see p 132). *2 Curved St., off Temple Bar. www1. cineworld.ie. ☎ 01/679-6716. Map p 126.*

★★ **Irish Film Institute** TEMPLE BAR   This arthouse film institute is a hip Temple Bar hangout for Dublin cinephiles. It houses three cinemas, the Irish Film Archive, a library, a small but comprehensive bookshop, and a cafe that's a good place for a cup of coffee on a cold afternoon. There's also a busy bar. Most cinema tickets run €8 to €10. *Wild Strawberries* is a bimonthly film club for the over 55s; see a classic movie with free tea or coffee. There are also special film-related events, many of which are free. *6 Eustace St. www.ifi.ie. ☎ 01/679-5744. Map p 126.*

★★ **Light House Cinema** SMITHFIELD   This lovely little cinema is one of the best venues in

Concert at 3Arena.

the city for independent and arthouse releases. It also regularly shows live HD broadcasts of theater, ballet, and opera from around the world, including the Bolshoi and the Royal Shakespeare Company. Tickets cost around €7 to €10. *Market Sq., Smithfield. www.light housecinema.ie.* ☎ *01/879-7601. Map p 125.*

★ **Savoy** O'CONNELL STREET Dating from 1929, this is Dublin's oldest cinema. The loveable Savoy, just down from the Gresham Hotel on O'Connell Street, contains six screens, showing mainly new releases and blockbuster fare. Expect to pay €9 to €14. *17 Upper O'Connell St. www.imccinemas.ie.* ☎ *01/874-8822. Map p 125.*

Pop, Rock & Jazz
★ **3Arena** NORTH WALL QUAY   This enormous indoor arena (known as **the O2** until

Music at Whelan's.

recently) is the biggest venue in Dublin, and the fifth-best-attended in the world at this writing. It's the go-to place for major international acts, standup comedy, and other big-ticket entertainment events—all top-of-the-bill stuff. *N. Wall Quay. www.3arena.ie.* ☎ *081/871-9300. Map p 125.*

★ **Olympia Theatre** TEMPLE BAR   Once Dating from 1879, this former music hall is instantly recognizable by the distinctive canopy over the front entrance, made of stained glass. These days it's mostly a music venue, attracting a host of top music acts in virtually every genre, plus occasional plays and big-ticket standup shows. Ticket prices vary hugely according to who's playing.*72 Dame St. www. olympia.ie.* ☎ *081/871-9330. Prices vary depending on the performer. Map p 126.*

★★ **Vicar Street** THE LIBERTIES This much-loved venue is definitely not Dublin's largest—its capacity is roughly ¼th that of the 3Arena (see above)—but it attracts consistently big names in music and standup comedy. Ticket prices vary. *58–59 Thomas St. www.vicarstreet.ie.* ☎ *01/775-5800. Map p 126.*

★★ **Whelan's** ST. STEPHEN'S GREEN   There are bands every night at this lively, two-level venue. Acts range from total unknowns to the hottest names in Irish music— not to mention international stars.

Advance Tickets & Listings

The tourism website www.ireland.com offers a handy "what's on" daily guide to cinema, theater, music, and whatever else you're up for—click "Destinations" and "Dublin City" from the front page, then follow the "Things to Do" link. You can search by type of experience or view complete events listings by date. The **Dublin Events Guide,** at www.dublinevents.com, also provides a comprehensive listing of the week's entertainment possibilities. As with any big city, ticket prices for shows vary considerably, from around €5 to over €100. Advance bookings for most large concerts, major plays, and so forth can be made through **Ticketmaster Ireland** (www.ticketmaster.ie; ☎ 81/871-9300 or 353/818-719-300 internationally, including Northern Ireland). The best way to arrange tickets is online or by phone, but if you prefer to speak to a human being in person, you can also drop by one of Ticketmaster's small Ticket Centres—central Dublin locations are at **Ticketron,** Jervis Shopping Centre, Jervis St., Dublin 1, and St. Stephen's Green Shopping Centre, St. Stephen's Green, Dublin 2; **FAI Umbro Store,** the Football Association of Ireland, 15 Westmoreland St., Dublin 2; and the Pavillion at **The Hub,** Dublin City University, Glasnevin.

Ticket prices vary according to who's playing. *25 Wexford St. www. whelanslive.com.* ☎ *01/478-0766. Map p 126.*

Spectator Sports
★★ **Aviva Stadium** BALLS-BRIDGE Entirely rebuilt and reopened in 2010, this is one of the main venues for sport in Ireland. Rugby and football (soccer) are the main attractions here. Expect to pay between €18 and €80 for a

Aviva Stadium.

ticket—and, unsurprisingly, the big home games can sell out well in advance. *62 Lansdowne Rd. www. avivastadium.ie.* ☎ *01/238-2300. Tickets from www.ticketmaster.ie. Map p 126.*

★★★ **Croke Park** DRUMCON-DRA Affectionately known as the Croker, this is the spiritual home of the two biggest sports in Ireland—Gaelic football and hurling, a kind of cross between hockey and soccer. There's no more essential place

A Year of Cultural Events

Each year kicks off in high-energy style, with **Funderland** (www.funderland.com; ☎ 01/283-8188), an annual indoor fun fair, complete with white-knuckle rides, carnival stalls, and family entertainment. In February the **Dublin International Film Festival** (www.jdiff.com; ☎ 01/662-4620) takes over the Irish Film Centre in Temple Bar. More than 100 films are featured, with screenings of the best in Irish and world cinema, plus seminars and lectures on filmmaking. Unsurprisingly, **St. Patrick's Day** is marked with parades galore and ample liquid refreshment (around Mar 17; www.stpatricksfestival.ie). Contemporary dancers from around the world take to various venues during the **World Irish Dancing Championships** in April (www.dublindancefestival.ie; ☎ 01/814-6298). In May, the 9-day **Dublin Writer's Fesitval** (www.dublinwriteresfestival.com; ☎ 01/222-5455) is one of the biggest events in the Irish literary calendar. High-profile authors from all over the world attend events at venues across the city. Also in May, gay contributors to the theater, past and present, are showcased in the **Dublin Gay Theatre Festival** (www.gaytheatre.ie). Majestic tall ships come sailing by in June's **Docklands Jamboree** (www.dublindocklands.ie; ☎ 01/818-3300) For 4 delicious days in June, **Taste of Dublin** (www.tasteofdublin.ie) comes to Temple Bar. Visitors can sample dishes prepared by some of the country's top chefs, and over 100 artisan producers. The event is usually a sellout, so booking is advisable. Also in June, the **Bloomsday Festival** celebrates Leopold Bloom, the central character of James Joyce's *Ulysses*. Every aspect of the city, including the menus at restaurants and pubs, duplicates the aromas, sights, sounds, and tastes of Joyce's fictitious Dublin on June 16, 1904, the day when all of the action in *Ulysses* takes place. Sports fans will want to try and bag a ticket to the **All-Ireland Hurling & Gaelic Football Finals** in September. The finals of Ireland's most beloved sports, hurling and Gaelic football, are Ireland's equivalent of the Super Bowl. If you can't be there live, experience this in the full bonhomie of a pub. In late September/early October, the **Dublin Theatre Festival** (www.dublintheatrefestival.com; ☎ 01/677-8439) showcases new plays by every major Irish company. In November the **Dublin Web Fest** (www.dublinwefest.com; ☎ 085/175-0360) comes to Filmbase in Temple Bar. The über-cool new festival, the first of its kind in Ireland, showcases the best in drama, comedy, and animation that has been independently produced for the web. Finally, in December, the winter wonderland that is **Dublin Docklands Christmas Festival** (www.docklnds.ie; ☎ 01/496-9883) rolls into town. Now part of the traditional run-up to Christmas in Dublin, this huge event all but takes over Docklands. Mostly it's an opportunity to shop (among some 100 different traders), but there's also a traditional-style fairground and festive food and drink aplenty.

Horse racing at Leopardstown.

to experience Irish sporting culture than among its roaring crowds. Ticket prices range from €15 to about €50. Like the Aviva Statium (see above), the Croker is sometimes used for major rock concerts. *Jones's Rd.* ☎ *01/865-8657. Season Apr–Sept. Tickets from www.ticket master.ie, www.gaa.ie, www.crokepark.ie.*

★ Leopardstown Racecourse

LEOPARDSTOWN   This popular track, with all-weather, glass-enclosed spectator stands, is 9.7km (6 miles) south of the city center. Racing meets—mainly steeplechases, but also a few flats—are scheduled two or three times a month throughout the year. Tickets run from about €20 to €40. *Foxrock. www.leopardstown.com.* ☎ *01/289-0500. Map p 126.*

★ Shelbourne Park RINGSEND

Dublin's main greyhound track, Shelbourne Park holds races all

Greyhound racing at Shelbourne Park.

year; check the website for current schedule. Expect to pay around €30 for a ticket. *Shelbourne Park. www.igb.ie.* ☎ *01/668-3502. Map p 126.*

Storytelling

★★★ An Evening of Food, Folkore & Fairies USHER'S

QUAY   The concept of this evening is timeless yet brilliant in its simplicity. No high-tech smoke and mirrors, just compelling tales from Irish folklore, passionately told by masters of the storytelling craft. To be clear, this is storytelling for all ages, not just children, and it's a brilliant revival of an ancient art. The whole thing takes place in an atmospherically lit room inside the **Brazen Head** pub (see p 117), one of the oldest pubs in Dublin. During dinner, the storytellers spin their absorbing yarns. The meal, which is included in the price, is suitably traditional as well: beef-and-Guinness stew or bacon and cabbage with mashed potatoes. If you haven't had your fill of Irish tradition by the end of it all, you can head downstairs and hear some live music in the bar. The storytelling evenings are held nightly at 7pm, all year (except in Jan and Feb, when it's only Thurs and Sat nights). Tickets cost €46 adults, €42 seniors and students, and €29 children (minimum age 6), including dinner. *The Brazen Head, 20 Lower Bridge St. www.irishfolktours.com.* ☎ *01/218-8555. Map p 126.*

Theaters & Venues

Abbey Theatre EDEN

QUAY   Since 1903, the Abbey has been the national theater of Ireland, and it remains one of the most respected and prestigious theaters in the country. The original theater, destroyed by fire in 1951, was replaced in 1966 by the current functional, if uninspired, 492-seat house. In addition to its main stage, the theater also has a 127-seat basement studio, the **Peacock,** where it presents newer, more experimental work. Tickets generally cost around €15 to €40. *26 Lower Abbey St., Dublin 1. www. abbeytheatre.ie.* ☎ *01/878-7222. Map p 125.*

★★ Bewley's Cafe Theatre

GRAFTON STREET   This excellent lunchtime theater has temporarily moved from its original venue while the Oriental Room at Bewley's is restored. The program mixes classic one-act plays by the likes of Oscar Wilde and George Bernard Shaw with brand-new work. You can order a light lunch to enjoy during the performance. Plays last no more than an hour. Tickets start at €8 (€12 if you want lunch). At this writing there's no word on when the

Gaiety Theatre.

restoration at Bewley's is likely to finish, so make sure you check the address of the venue. *Powerscourt Theatre at the Powerscourt Townhouse Centre, S. William St. www. bewleyscafetheatre.com.* ☎ *086/878-4001. Map p 126.*

★ Gaiety Theatre ST. STEPHEN'S GREEN   The elegant little Gaiety, opened in 1871, hosts a varied array of performances, everything from opera to classical Irish plays and Broadway-style musicals. (The Gaiety's annual pantomime, or Christmas show, is a big event in the city's theatrical calendar.) And when the thespians leave, the partygoers arrive: On Friday and Saturday from midnight on, the place turns into a nightclub, with four bars hosting live bands and DJs, spinning R&B, indie, blues, or hip hop. There are even occasional cult movie showings. Be sure to check out the ornate decor before you get too tipsy. Tickets prices vary considerably, from around €15 to €50. *S. King St. www.gaiety theatre.ie.* ☎ *01/677-1717. Map p 126.*

★ Gate Theatre PARNELL

SQUARE   Just north of O'Connell Street off Parnell Square, this recently restored 370-seat theater was founded in 1928 by Irish actors Hilton Edwards and Michael MacLiammoir to provide a venue for a broad range of plays; its program today still includes a blend of modern works and the classics. Although less known by visitors, the Gate is easily as distinguished as the Abbey. Tickets range from €20 to €30. *1 Cavendish Row. www. gate-theatre.ie.* ☎ *01/874-4045. Map p 125.* ●

Lodging **Best Bets**

Most **Historic Bedroom**
★★★ The Shelbourne $$$$ 27 St. Stephen's Green (p 146)

Best **Aparthotel**
★★ The Merchant House $$$ 8 Eustace St. (p 145)

Best **Temple Bar Hideaway**
★★ The Clarence $$$ 6–8 Wellington Quay (p 142)

Best **City Center Bargain**
★★ Harding Hotel $$$ Copper Alley, Fishamble St. (p 144)

Most **Friendly Hotel Cat**
★ Aberdeen Lodge $$$ 53–55 Park Ave., Ballsbridge (p 140)

Best **Suburban Charmer**
★★★ Ariel House $$$ 50–54 Lansdowne Rd., Ballsbridge (p 140)

Best **High-End Bargain**
★★ The Gresham $$$ 23 O'Connell St. (p 144)

Best **for Fashionistas**
★★ The Morrison $$$ 8 Lower Ormond Quay (p 146)

Best **for Shopaholics**
★★★ The Westbury $$$$$ Grafton St. (p 147)

Most **Imaginative Restoration**
★★ Westin $$$$ Westmoreland St. (p 148)

Best **Out-of-Town Retreat**
★★★ The White Cottages $$ Balbriggan Rd., Skerries (p 148)

North Dublin Lodging

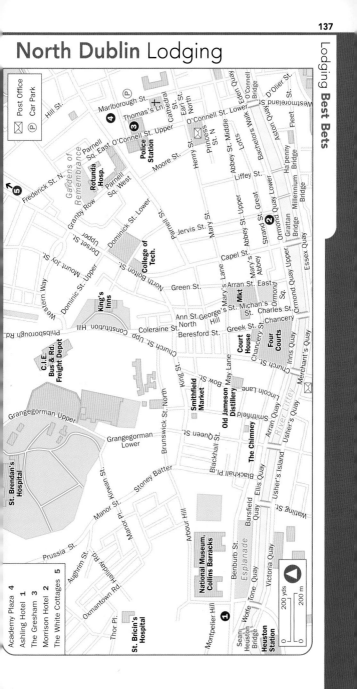

Post Office

ⓟ Car Park

Academy Plaza **4**
Ashling Hotel **1**
The Gresham **3**
Morrison Hotel **2**
The White Cottages **5**

South Dublin Lodging

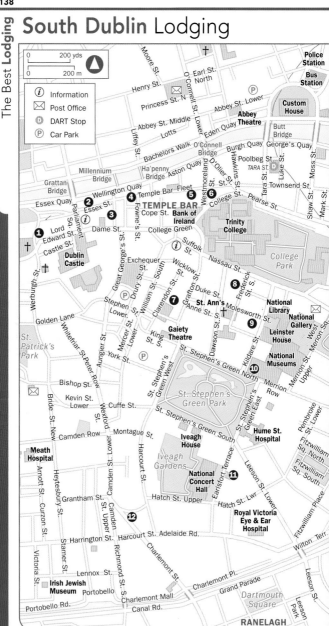

Legend:
- (i) Information
- ✉ Post Office
- Ⓓ DART Stop
- Ⓟ Car Park

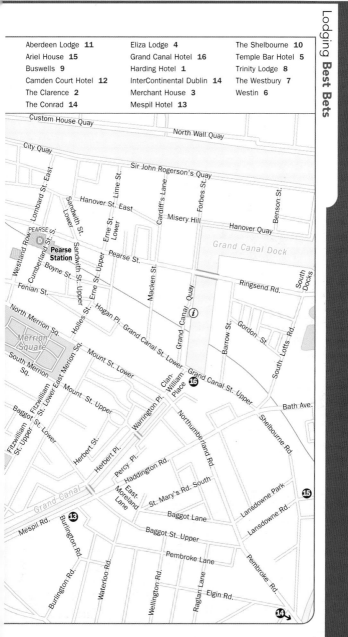

Dublin Lodging A to Z

★ Aberdeen Lodge BALLS-BRIDGE   Drive up to this elegant Regency building in the springtime, and its front is so covered in ivy, it looks like a vertical lawn with spaces cut for the windows. Inside, the decor is endearingly old-fashioned; neat-as-a-pin public spaces have heavy, antique-style furnishings and embroidered pillows scattered hither and thither. Guest rooms are comfortable and quiet, if a little plain, but modern bathrooms are a big plus. Some have views of the large garden, where guests can take tea, often in the company of the hotel's friendly cat. Aberdeen Lodge is a short walk to the nearest DART station, and from here it's a short hop to the city center. *53–55 Park Ave., Ballsbridge. www.aberdeen-lodge.com.* ☎ *01/283-8155. 11 units. €162–€185 double. DART: Sydney Parade, Sandymount. Bus: 2, 3, 18. Map p 138.*

★★ Academy Plaza CITY CENTER   Owned by the Best Western chain, this large, modern, low-frills option is popular with business travelers but well located for travelers exploring central Dublin. The lobby is small but pleasant, with wood paneling and leather furniture; rooms are compact and simple, with cream walls, rust-and-brown-colored carpet, and windows well-insulated from the street noise. Some rooms are bigger than others, so if size matters, request a deluxe room. Bathrooms are decent and modern, with showers above the baths. Breakfasts are sizeable, if not terribly varied, and can be ordered in your room (for a charge). The staff is pleasant, and the location, for the money, is very good. *10–14 Findlater Place, off O'Connell St. www.academy plazahotel.ie.* ☎ *01/878-0666. 304 units. €87–€149 double. Luas: Abbey St. Bus: inc. 2, 3, 4. Map p 137.*

★★★ Ariel House BALLS-BRIDGE   This charming guest-house in Ballsbridge has won several plaudits over the last few years. And rightly so—it's a smoothly run, great value-for-the-money operation, situated on a quiet Victorian street. The most obvious landmark you can see, depending on your point of view, is either a hideous blot or a great day out—the Aviva Stadium, one of Ireland's major sports grounds, literally a block away. Inside the hotel, the vibe is decidedly old-school, with a subtle contemporary flourish. The small, simple guest rooms are tastefully decorated in

Sitting room at Ariel House.

The Ashling Hotel.

earthy oatmeal or cream with brocade-pattern bedspreads. The lounge is a pleasant space with an honesty bar; musically inclined guests are even free to tickle the ivories of the piano. The breakfast menu doesn't veer too far from the traditional Irish staples, but it's exceptionally well done. So long as you're not staying on a match day, the neighborhood is quiet enough to make you feel tucked away from the crowds, but with good transport links to central Dublin. *50–54 Lansdowne Rd., Ballsbridge. www.ariel-house.net.* ☎ *01/668-5512. 37 units. €130–€180 double. Parking (free). DART: Lansdowne Road Bus: 4, 7, 8, 84. Map p 138.*

★ **Ashling Hotel** SMITHFIELD The Ashling is a quality affordable option, close to several attractions on the eastern end of the city center. Guestrooms are modern and fairly spacious, though it's worth paying the extra for a deluxe room with better views of the city. There's a good restaurant offering classic Irish dishes, and a daily lunchtime "carvery" (roast meat, again served buffet style). Special offers include package deals that cover entry to local attractions. Central Dublin is a 10-minute tram ride, or a 25-minute walk. This is also the last stop on the Airlink coach (see p 167) before the airport, so the location has advantages. *Parkgate St. www.ashlinghotel. ie. ☎ 01/677-2324. 225 units.*

€134–€210 double. Luas: Museum. Bus: inc. 25, 26, 66. Map p 137.

★★ **Buswells** CITY CENTER The traditional air of a gentleman's club prevails at this midpriced hotel in central Dublin. Original features of the Georgian building are maintained, from the intricate cornices of the 19th-century plasterwork to the polished marble fireplaces and heavy curtains. Therefore it can come as a surprise to find that the small but decently furnished guest rooms are modern in style (rather bland, even, after the lovely, traditional spaces one walks through to get to them). Visitors with mobility problems should ask for a room on a lower floor, as the old building (actually three townhouses merged together) is full of stairs to climb. Pleasant though it is, Buswell's real selling point is its location—just a few minutes' walk to Trinity College in one direction and St. Stephen's Green in the other. You're in the very heart of the action here. *23–25 Molesworth St. www.buswells.ie.* ☎ *01/614-6500. 69 units. €141–€209 double. DART: Pearse. Bus: inc. 11, 13, 14. Map p 138.*

★★ **Camden Court Hotel** ST. STEPHEN'S GREEN Although not exactly budget, this large hotel just south of St. Stephen's Green is great value for what you get. A "practical base" kind of hotel, rather than one overflowing with character and charm, the Camden

Lobby of Buswells.

Court is nonetheless well equipped, with good-size, modern guest rooms (especially the family rooms), a pool, and a massage salon to soothe away a few of those sightseeing aches and pains. You'd pay significantly more if this place was just a few blocks farther north; the only real drawback is that you're a 10- to 20-minute walk away from the center. *Camden St. Lower (near junction with Charlotte Way). www.camdencourthotel.com.* ☎ *01/475-9666. 246 units. €165–€220 double. Luas: Harcourt St. Bus: 19, 83, 122. Map p 138.*

★★ **The Clarence** CITY CENTER/ TEMPLE BAR   Back in the 1990s, when the Celtic Tiger was starting to roar, the Clarence became something of a symbol of the "new" Dublin. Chic, fashionable, and with megastar owners to boot (Bono and the Edge from U2), it spoke of Dublin's revival as a modern and cultured capital city. These days, with the economy slowing down, the Clarence has lost some of its original luster—U2 have sold their share, and a refurbishment is overdue in places. The surrounding profusion of trendy bars and restaurants also means that street noise is a problem (despite what they all tell you, no hotel smack-dab

in the middle of the capital's party district can ever *really* guarantee a quiet night's sleep). That said, the friendly and professional staff goes a long way toward making up for the disappointing edges. Pleasant, well-sized guest rooms are done in contemporary tones (chocolate and cream or white with accents of scarlet and black). Most of the furniture is the work of Irish designers, and beds are luxuriously comfortable. And a definite plus is the price tag—rooms here are relative bargains, considering that this still qualifies as a big-name hotel in the city. The trendy (and pricey) **Cleaver East** restaurant serves ultra-contemporary Irish cuisine, and stopping by the **Octagon Bar** for a pint of Guinness is a must, even if you're not staying. *6-8 Wellington Quay. www.theclarence.ie.* ☎ *01/407-0800. 49 units. €179–€260 double. Bus: 26, 66, 67. Map p 138.*

★★ **The Conrad** ST. STEPHEN'S GREEN   The Dublin outpost of Hilton's high-end brand is all about the luxury. Beds in the spacious, modern guest rooms are sumptuously comfortable (and refreshingly large for a European hotel, even in the cheapest rooms). Color schemes of chocolate and cream, or oatmeal and royal blue, convey an air of elegance without feeling too fussy. Thoughtful touches, such as Nespresso machines in every room, are welcome—although charging for something as basic as Wi-Fi, when almost every good B&B in the city now provides it for free, is parsimonious. Despite all the luxury, this place certainly feels geared more toward business travelers than anyone else. The excellent **Alex** restaurant, specializing in seafood, is well worth a splurge. *Earlsfort Terrace. conrad hotels3.hilton.com.* ☎ *01/602-8900. 191 units. €215–€599 double. Bus: 126. Map p 138.*

★ **Eliza Lodge** TEMPLE BAR Right in the middle of Temple Bar, above a popular Italian restaurant and overlooking the River Liffey, this smart hotel could hardly feel more in the thick of the action. Guest rooms are simple and compact, with large windows letting in plenty of natural light, although the modern bathrooms can verge on shoebox size. Like so many other hotels in this neighborhood, however, its biggest drawback is the flip side of its greatest asset: the location. Temple Bar is the liveliest part of a busy capital city, and the fact that Eliza Lodge is also on a major traffic intersection hardly acts as an aid to restful sleep. That's good enough reason to fork over extra

for an upper-floor room, which also gets you a better view of the river. *23–24 Wellington Quay (on the corner of Eustace St.). www.elizalodge. com.* ☎ *01/671-8044. 18 units. €179–€329 double. Bus: inc. 26, 51, 79. Map p 138.*

★ **Grand Canal Hotel** BALLS-BRIDGE Overlooking the 18th-century Grand Canal—a major part of Dublin's industrial heritage, long since abandoned as anything but a picturesque waterway—this large hotel is a strikingly modern place. As with many hotels in this neighborhood, you can't escape the looming carbuncle of the Aviva Stadium, and this modern hotel is a particular favorite of sports fans in town for a game. But it's also a haven for business travelers and tourists looking for a pleasant place to stay. The hotel is cheerful, spotlessly clean, and the bedrooms are huge by Dublin standards. The city center is a just short journey by public transport. You could even walk if you wanted to work off one of the hearty hotel breakfasts—Trinity College is about 20 minutes on foot. *Grand Canal St. Upper, Ballsbridge. www.grandcanalhotel.ie.* ☎ *01/646-1000. 142 units. €95–€162 double. DART: Grand Canal Dock. Bus: 4, 5, 7, 7A, 8, 45, 63, 84. Map p 138.*

Family room at Camden Court Hotel.

★★ **The Gresham** O'CONNELL STREET   One of Dublin's most historic hotels, the Gresham is also one of the oldest—it opened in 1817, though it was almost destroyed during the Easter Rising of 1916. Most of the current building dates from the 1920s, the public areas retain a glamorous Art Deco feel, preserved during a big modernization of the hotel in the mid-2000s. Although the suites are nothing short of opulent, the cheaper guest rooms are really quite basic—but they're comfortable, quiet, and, most important, surprisingly affordable for a hotel with this kind of pedigree. The **Writer's Lounge,** a beautiful remnant of its Jazz Age heyday, is a popular spot for afternoon tea. Overlooking both the hotel lobby and busy O'Connell Street, it's a good perch for people-watching. The main O'Connell Street taxi rank is directly outside, and it's about a 15-minute walk to Temple Bar. *23 Upper O'Connell St. www.gresham-hotels.com.* ☎ *01/874-6881. 298 units. €90–€265 double. Luas: Abbey St. Bus: inc. 2, 3, 4. Map p 137.*

★★ **Harding Hotel** CITY CENTER   Just central enough not to feel like a trek to the main tourist sites, but far enough to escape the inevitable nighttime crowds that descend on nearby Temple Bar, this is an excellent option on the western edge of the city center. The polished wood and bright, floor-to-ceiling windows of the cheerful lobby give off a pleasantly old-fashioned vibe, even though most of the hotel is quite modern. The comfortable guest rooms are a terrific value. Even in high season, you can usually find a double room for well under €100, and triple rooms typically cost just a little bit more than standard doubles. This makes the Harding a particularly standout option for families. It's not overly fancy, but it's pleasant, clean, and has everything you need. *Copper Alley, Fishamble St. www.harding hotel.ie.* ☎ *01/679-6500. 52 units. €87–€131 double. Bus: inc. 37, 39, 49. Map p 138.*

★★ **InterContinental Dublin** BALLSBRIDGE   This purpose-built, modern hotel has been designed in a traditional style, more redolent of a country house than you'd think from the imposing brick-and-glass exterior. From the elegantly simple guest rooms, with their sumptuously comfortable beds, to the outstanding full-service spa, the hotel offers a host of thoughtful touches. The spa is excellent; look for discount packages that include massage treatments. The only real

Suite at the Grand Canal Hotel.

"Subject to Availability"

During popular events like international rugby matches, major pop concerts, and St. Patrick's Day, prices leap up and availability goes down, so bear this in mind if your dates are flexible. The flip side is that luxury hotels often have good deals during off-peak times, especially on weekends, particularly via their own websites. Wherever you intend staying and whenever you visit, it's worth booking as far ahead as possible.

downside is the location. Views over the rooftops of Ballsbridge are never going to appeal as much as the kind of vista you get at high-end establishments in the city center—but the payoff is greater peace and quiet. (It's only a short train or taxi ride into the center anyway.) *Simmonscourt Rd., Ballsbridge. www. intercontinental.com/dublin.* ☎ *01/665-4000. 195 units. €283– €390 double. DART: Sandymount. Bus: 4, 7, 8. Map p 138.*

★★ **The Merchant House** CITY CENTER Mainly geared toward business travelers and couples, the accommodations here are different from that of a conventional guesthouse. The Merchant House is a series of swanky guest suites, with various services attached but no dedicated reception area. The upside to this is a greater degree of privacy and freedom. The downside is that, while the entrance is secure and private, the building isn't staffed all the time. (Travelers who prefer their local color not too, well, colorful, should also be warned that it's next door to a fetish store— albeit a fairly discreet one.) The suites themselves are extremely well designed; features of the original 18th-century building were beautifully retained when the place was renovated in 2006. Nicely modern touches include flatscreen TVs

and elegant contemporary furnishings, and fancy optional extras include a dedicated chauffeur. The bed-and-breakfast rate includes daily housekeeping service and breakfast at a nearby cafe. No children allowed. *8 Eustace St. www. themerchanthouse.eu.* ☎ *01/633-4447. 4 units. €120–€145 double. Bus: inc. 39B, 49X, 50X. Map p 138.*

★ **Mespil Hotel** BALLSBRIDGE Another reasonable option in Ballsbridge, the Mespil is about a 15-minute walk from St. Stephen's Green. Accommodations here are certainly of a higher standard than what you're likely to find uptown for the same price. (Stays of more than one night usually qualify for discounts if you book online). The guest rooms are spacious and feature modern decor and comfortable beds. In common with most

Bram Stoker Suite at the Merchant House.

hotels of this type, breakfast is served buffet style—tasty and excellent fuel, to be sure, although all that fried meat and eggs gets wearing after a couple of days. One nice little bonus: An excellent gourmet food market is held just outside by the canal, every Thursday from 11am to 2pm. See **www.irishvillagemarkets.com** for more details. *50–60 Mespil Rd. www.mespilhotel.com.* ☎ *01/448-4600. 255 units. €159–€189 double. Bus: inc. 10, 15X, 49X. Map p 138.*

★★ **The Morrison** O'CONNELL STREET   Rooms at this chic hotel on the north bank of the Liffey verge on futuristic, with ultra-modern furniture, moody uplighting, and a host of flashy extras, such as 40-inch HDTVs. It's all very straight lines and fancy gizmos (they even have in-house tech support), although song lyrics painted onto the walls here and there add an edge of Irish literary romance. There's a good restaurant, the **Morrison Grill**, and a funky cocktail lounge. Sometimes it can feel a little like form over function, but the helpful staff makes everything run smoothly. *Lower Ormond Quay. www.morrisonhotel.ie.* ☎ *01/887-2400. 138 units. €246–€410 double. Bus: inc. 25, 66, 67. Map p 137.*

★★★ **The Shelbourne** ST. STEPHEN'S GREEN   Dublin hotels simply don't come with a better

historic pedigree than this—the Irish Constitution was written in this very building (room 112, to be precise). The Shelbourne was acquired by the Marriott group a few years ago, but traditionalists need not fear, because the hotel is still its grand old self. Most of the old wrinkles were ironed out courtesy of a major refurbishment in 2007. A feeling of *fin de siècle* elegance pervades throughout the public areas, with high plaster ceilings, crystal chandeliers, and a winding iron staircase. Guest rooms have a much more discreet, contemporary elegance, with extremely luxurious beds and a host of modern extras. There's also an excellent spa, and you can even book a session with a Genealogy Butler if you need a little expert help in tracing your Irish roots. Afternoon tea at the Shelbourne is a true Dublin institution; consider splurging on a booking, even if you can't spring for a night here. *27 St. Stephen's Green. www.marriott.co.uk.* ☎ *01/663-4500. 190 units. €332–€540 doubleLuas: St. Stephen's Green. Bus: inc. 10, 11, 14. Map p 138.*

★★ **Temple Bar Hotel** TEMPLE BAR   This cheerful, well-run hotel certainly wins in the location stakes, sitting right in the middle of trendy Temple Bar. Guest rooms are surprisingly large, decorated in a clean, modern style, albeit with

Guest room at the Mespil Hotel.

Guest room in the Morrison.

rather cheap furnishings. Executive rooms offer plenty of extra space for a small premium. The bar downstairs has live music, although if it's not to your fancy, there are a dozen other lively pubs within a stone's throw. The amenities are somewhat lacking for the price, but then again this *is* Temple Bar—hardly bargain central around here. *10 Fleet St. www.templebarhotel.com.* ☎ *01/612-9200. 129 units. €190–€276 double. DART: Pearse. Bus: 100X, 133. Map p 138.*

★ **Trinity Lodge** ST. STEPHEN'S GREEN   This small hotel is full of quirks—not all of them convenient (there's no elevator and plenty of stairs, for instance)—but the bedrooms are comfortable, contemporary, and surprisingly large for a place in this price range. A converted townhouse, the hotel was built in 1785, and some of the bedrooms retain a historic feel to the design. Quadruple rooms offer outstanding value for families. South Frederick Street is little more than a stone's throw from Trinity College; it's also—a comparative rarity in the city center—generally quite peaceful at night. Breakfast is Continental and "express style" (translation: basic), but the neighborhood has plenty of other options. *12 S. Frederick St. www.trinitylodge.com.* ☎ *01/617-0900. 16 units. €180–€285 double. Rail: Connolly. Luas: St. Stephen's Green. DART: Pearse. Bus: inc. 10, 11, 15. Map p 138.*

★★★ **The Westbury** ST. STEPHEN'S GREEN   Virtually made for well-heeled shopaholics, this top-end hotel on Grafton Street is a luxurious and stylish retreat. Bedrooms are huge and modern, with subtle floral wallpaper, handmade furniture, and soothing beige and cream tones. Beds are comfortable (although with so much space to spare, they could be bigger), and a few are modern-style fourposters. **Wilde,** the excellent Modern Irish restaurant, is a beautiful space overlooking Grafton Street; it also serves one of the city's finest afternoon teas. There's also a more relaxed bar and bistro. Check the website for some enticing package deals, including dinner/bed-and-breakfast and theater options. *Grafton St. www.doylecollection.com.* ☎ *01/602-8900. 205 units. €249–€374 double. Bus: inc. 11, 14, 15A. Map p 138.*

The Westbury Hotel, on Grafton Street.

Getting the Best Rate

There isn't much point in quoting a "rack rate" in this chapter (the hotels' published price); instead, it's more useful to put the commonly available minimum price for a standard double, ranged with the hotel's own "standard" price. You'll rarely have to pay the rack rate at top hotels if booking in advance, and only when you request a specific date will you get a price. For the best discounts at top hotels, check their own websites, as they often offer good discounts and packages especially in low season, on weekends, and away from major events (see "Subject to Availability," above). It's also worth checking out discounts at booking websites like **www.hotels.com** and **www.booking.com**; that luxury topnotch hotel might actually be more affordable. In most instances, the cheapest rates do not include breakfast.

★★ The Westin CITY CENTER

With its grand, imposing facade (thanks to its former incarnation as a bank), this hotel boasts an interior with some handsome original 19th-century features, and even those parts that feel more modern have an impeccably well-maintained elegance to them. Guest rooms are large and have a refined modern decor, with subtly distressed wood furniture and wide leather headboards on outrageously comfortable beds. The **Mint Bar** remains a fashionable hangout for the Dublin glitterati, and the basement **Exchange** restaurant serves excellent contemporary European food. The only thing missing is a spa, but you can book pampering treatments in your room. *Westmoreland St. www.thewestindublin.com.* ☎ *01/645-1000. 163 units. €310–€400 double. Bus: inc. 1, 9, 11. Map p 138.*

★★★ The White Cottages

SKERRIES   The sea is an ever-present feature at this pleasant, whitewashed little B&B in Skerries, a pretty commuter town just north of Dublin. The coastline is literally feet away from the wooden terrace at the back, and the sound of the waves can help soothe you to a restful sleep at night. Guest rooms are decorated in summery white and blue colors, with jaunty, candy-striped accents. The owners are welcoming and extremely helpful—Joe, the co-owner, is a mine of information about the local area, and his wife Jackie displays some of her art around the house. Breakfasts are good, and in summer you can get afternoon tea (€20) or a "romantic picnic" lunch (€25), although you have to fend for yourself at dinnertime. (Joe can provide an exhaustive list of places to eat nearby.) The only major snag is that Skerries is far outside of the city; the train journey to the center takes about 40 minutes, and the bus over an hour. Still, it's nothing more than local commuters do every day, and you'll be hard pressed to find a more tranquil and welcoming retreat after a long day's sightseeing. *Balbriggan Rd., Skerries, Co. Dublin. www.thewhitecottages.com.* ☎ *01/849-2231. 4 units. €90 double. Rail: Skerries. Bus: 33. Map p 137.* ●

Powerscourt Estate & Gardens

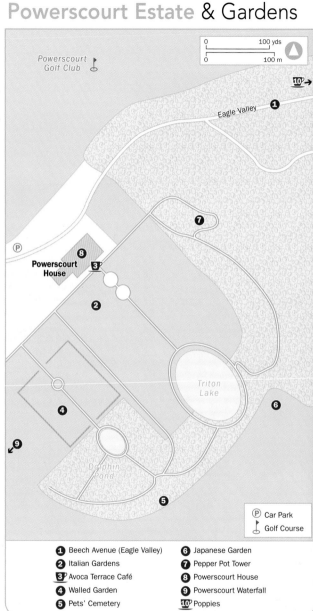

| 0 | 100 yds |
| 0 | 100 m |

Powerscourt Golf Club

10 →

Eagle Valley **1**

7

Ⓟ

8

Powerscourt House

3 Avoca Terrace Café

2

Triton Lake

6

4

9

Dolphin Pond

5

Ⓟ Car Park

🏌 Golf Course

1 Beech Avenue (Eagle Valley)
2 Italian Gardens
3 Avoca Terrace Café
4 Walled Garden
5 Pets' Cemetery
6 Japanese Garden
7 Pepper Pot Tower
8 Powerscourt House
9 Powerscourt Waterfall
10 Poppies

Previous page: Dun Laoghaire Harbour.

I n the shadow of Big Sugar Loaf Mountain in Wicklow, the Powerscourt Estate has statue-studded lawns & secluded pathways. Originally a 14th-century castle, the house has been altered greatly over time; it was rebuilt by Richard Wingfield and his ancestors from 1603 and gutted by fire in 1974. The newly restored house is imposing, but the formal gardens are the real jewels. START: **See box, "Practical Matters."**

❶ ★★ Beech Avenue (Eagle Valley). This is a case where "getting there" really is half the fun. This tranquil walk from Enniskerry takes you along the mile-long avenue lined by more than 2,000 beech trees. It's lovely in summer, but stunning in fall, when the leaves turn a vivid shade of red. There's barely a car in sight, and few signs to reassure you that yes, you are on the right road. Enjoy your first glimpse of the Wicklow Mountains on your left as you approach the house.

❷ ★★ Italian Gardens. This grandiose section of the grounds was commissioned by the sixth Viscount Powerscourt in the 1840s and designed by architect Daniel Robertson, a proponent of Italianate gardens. Suffering from gout, Robertson allegedly directed operations to the 100 workers from a wheelbarrow while fortified by a bottle of sherry. When the bottle ran out, work ended for the day. Thankfully it all paid off. Your best views are from the upper terrace down to the mosaic patterned staircase with pebbles from nearby Bray, past 6th-century statues of Apollo, Diana, and Cupid, vases copied from Versailles, and dazzling green lawns with beds of deep-red roses. At the bottom, a pair of life-size winged Pegasus horses made from zinc guard the lily-filled Triton pond, framed perfectly by the landscaped slopes and the 501m- (1,644-ft.) high peak of Big Sugar Loaf.

❸ Avoca Terrace Cafe. Homemade cakes, soups, sandwiches, tarts, and a host of other delicious nibbles are to be enjoyed here, with a simply breathtaking view of the Wicklow Mountains to boot. ☎ 01-204 6070. $.

Italian Gardens and Triton Lake, Powerscourt Estate.

Triton Lake, Powerscort House and Gardens.

4 ★ Walled Garden. Dating back to 1740, this is one of Powerscourt's oldest features. As you enter through the elaborate Chorus Gates decorated with bugling angels, the aroma of the fragrant rose beds wafts over. Look for the memorial to Julia, 7th Viscountess Powerscourt, who died in 1931. She was obviously a fan of the Renaissance man, as the fountain is embellished with four busts of great Italian masters.

5 ★★ Pets' Cemetery. Powerscourt's owners become more endearing at this resting place for the beloved animals of the Wingfield and Slazenger families (Powerscourt's past and current owners). It's not unusual for well-loved pets to be buried in marked graves in Ireland, but this is thought to be the country's largest private pets' cemetery. Pay your respects to Sailor, the curly retriever and faithful companion for 5 years (died 1909); Tommy, a Shetland pony who died in 1936 aged 32, and his companion Magic; and the Jersey cow Eugenie who had 17 calves and produced over 100,000 gallons of milk.

6 ★★ Japanese Garden. Laid out half a century after the Italian Gardens (**2**) and built on reclaimed bogland, this garden has concentric paths leading to dazzling red Japanese maples and tiny bridges over a stream. It's very much a European pastiche of Asian styles, complete with Chinese fortune palms and pagoda—but the effect is rather charming. Nearby, look out for the 18th-century grotto with water cascading over fossilized sphagnum moss, found on the banks of the River Dargle.

7 ★ Pepper Pot Tower. The eastern section of the gardens is dominated by the fairytale-like

Powerscourt's Japanese Garden.

Practical Matters: Powerscourt

Organized bus trips from Dublin drop you at the gates, but it's more fun (and cheaper) on public transport. Catch the DART to coastal Bray (40 min; for basic transport information, see also *Dún Laoghaire*, p 154), and then bus no. 185 to Enniskerry village from outside the station (15 min). It's approximately a 1½ mile walk, from the village and turning right along Eagle Valley, to the main entrance of the gardens. Open daily 9:30am to 5:30pm; gardens close at dusk in winter. Admission: €8.50 adults; €7.50 seniors and students; €5 children 15 and under. www.powerscourt.ie. ☎ 01-204 6000.

tower that rises from the surrounding conifers, built to commemorate the 1911 visit of the Prince of Wales (later King Edward VIII—for just 11 months in 1939). It's shaped like the 8th Viscount's pepper pot, and you can climb to the top for views of the grounds. Follow in the footsteps of the Viscount and stroll through the surrounding woodland, known as his "private walk and American Garden" because of the rare plants from North America.

8 ★ Powerscourt House. It's hard to match the outstanding vistas and collection of gardens, so the recently restored house might be a bit of a disappointment. It's home to a stylish shopping gallery (mainly with the Irish interior designs of Avoca). Inside the house, an exhibition has photographs showing the history of the building and how the entrance hall looked before the fire, complete with antlers and stucco ceiling and cluttered with Victorian furniture. The historic ballroom is now a prestigious venue for society weddings and dinners and is open to the public until 1:30pm on Sundays and Mondays in summer (Sun only in winter, except for private parties).

9 ★ Powerscourt Waterfall. If you're feeling energetic, follow the well-marked path over 7km (4 miles) to this picturesque waterfall—the highest in Ireland at 121m (397 ft.). Or you can drive, following signs from the estate. ⏱ *30 min (without the walk). Admission €5.50 adults, €5 seniors & students, €2.50 children 15 & under, €6 families. May–Aug 9:30am–7pm; Mar–Apr & Sept–Oct 10:30am–5:30pm; Nov–Feb 10:30am–4:30pm.*

10 Poppies. This is a great pit stop for a cheap and cheerful lunch in Enniskerry, a few minutes' drive or a manageable walk from Powerscourt. Don't expect anything fancy, but it's all freshly made—panini, sandwiches, salads, quiches, and meat pies. The shepherd's pie is a local favorite. Treat yourself to one of the delicious cakes for dessert. You can also get anything on the menu to go. *The Square, Enniskerry. www.poppies.ie.* ☎ *01-282 8869. $.*

Dún Laoghaire to Dalkey

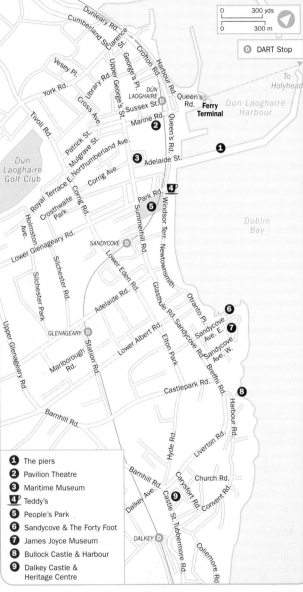

| 0 | 300 yds |
| 0 | 300 m |

D DART Stop

Dunleary Rd.
Cumberland St.
Clarence St.
George's Pl.
Crofton Rd.
Harbour Rd.
Vesey Pl.
Upper George's St.
York Rd.
Library Rd.
Cross Ave.
DÚN LAOGHAIRE
Sussex St.
Tivoli Rd.
Marine Rd.
Queen's Rd.
Ferry Terminal
Dún Laoghaire Harbour
To Holyhead

Dún Laoghaire Golf Club

Patrick St.
Mulgrave St.
Northumberland Ave.
Adelaide St.
Corrig Ave.
Royal Terrace E.
Crosthwaite Park
Corrig Rd.
Park Rd.
Windsor Terr.
Newtownsmith
Dublin Bay

Holmston Ave.
Lower Glenageary Rd.
Summerhill Rd.
SANDYCOVE **D**
Glasthule Rd.
Otranto Pl.
Sandycove Rd.
Sandycove Ave. E.
Sandycove Ave. W.

Silchester Rd.
Silchester Park
Lower Eden Rd.
Adelaide Rd.
GLENAGEARY **D**
Station Rd.
Lower Albert Rd.
Elton Park
Breffni Rd.
Castlepark Rd.

Upper Glenageary Rd.
Marlborough Rd.
Harbour Rd.
Liverton Rd.

Barnhill Rd.
Hyde Rd.
Church Rd.
Carysfort Rd.
Convent Rd.

Barnhill Rd.
Dalkey Ave.
Castle St.
Tubbermore Rd.
DALKEY **D**
Coliemore Rd.

1. The piers
2. Pavilion Theatre
3. Maritime Museum
4. Teddy's
5. People's Park
6. Sandycove & The Forty Foot
7. James Joyce Museum
8. Bullock Castle & Harbour
9. Dalkey Castle & Heritage Centre

Formerly known as Kingstown, in honor of King George IV's visit, the port town of Dún Laoghaire (pronounced "Dun-Leery") is a popular day trip. It's a bracing coastal walk from here to Sandycove for seal watching or even a swim, and on to the swanky suburb of Dalkey. The hardy can continue to Killiney's golden beaches, or, if you don't fancy the walk, Dún Laoghaire alone is a great day out—especially on weekends. START: **DART to Dún Laoghaire.**

1 ★★ **The piers.** The west and east piers, popular promenading spots, jut out among the yachts, fishing boats, and huge Holyhead passenger ferry. A touch of sunshine brings everyone onto the walkways, with families, roller-bladers, and joggers striding out. If you return here at the end of the day, the place is likely to be packed.

2 ★ **Pavilion Theatre.** This excellent seaside theater has a bit of everything, from touring plays to concerts and films. There's a strong program of children's plays and family entertainment, with some matinee shows, so it might be worth checking the listings to see what's on if you're here with kids. *Marine Rd. www.paviliontheatre.ie.* ☎ *01-231 2929.*

3 ★★ **Maritime Museum.** Housed in the 1837 **Mariner's Church,** this museum charts Ireland's maritime heritage. Highlights of the permanent collection include the Baily Optic, the 2-million-candlepower lamp from the Howth lighthouse, in use from 1902 to 1972 (it still works); an exhibition devoted to the ill-fated SS *Titanic*; and a reconstructed early radio room. There are gorgeous views of the harbor from the bell tower when the sun is shining. ⏱ *45 min. Haigh Terrace. www.mariner.ie.* ☎ *01-280 0969. Admission €5 adults, €3 children 11 & under, €12 families. Tues–Sat 11am–5pm.*

4 **kids** **Teddy's.** There's a wonderfully nostalgic feel to this old-fashioned ice cream bar, which is something of a local institution. They also sell a positively Wonka-esque variety of candy. *1A Windsor Terrace.* ☎ *086-452 9394. $.*

Kayaking in Dún Laoghaire.

Practical Matters: Dún Laoghaire

Located 12km (8 miles) south of Dublin, Dún Laoghaire is easily accessed by the speedy DART train. Jump on at Connolly, Tara Street, Pearse, or Grand Canal Dock stations, with a round-trip ticket for €6.15. Services run approximately every 10 to 15 minutes Monday to Saturday (6:15am–midnight); and every 30 minutes Sunday (9am–midnight). Info line: ☎ 1850-366 222; 24-hour talking timetable: ☎ 1890-77 88 99. The **Tourist Information Office** (☎ 01-280 6964) is located at the Dún Laoghaire County Hall on Marine Road. It's open daily 10am to 1:30pm and 2:30pm to 5pm, with reduced hours in winter.

⑤ ★ People's Park. This small park just outside the town center is pleasant enough to wander through, but every Sunday people crowd here for the weekly **Farmer's Market.** Local and regional produce is for sale, and there are always stalls selling hot food to go. *Market: Sun 10am–5pm.*

⑥ ★★ Sandycove & The Forty Foot. This tiny cove of golden sand is a haven for families

Learing to sail in Dún Laoghaire.

and anyone seeking precious sun—so not surprisingly it's packed during warm weekends. The historic Forty Foot, once a "Gentleman's bathing place" (i.e., nude) now accepts women swimmers. A chilly dip even in summer, this is the venue for a traditional Christmas Day swim for the truly hardy. Look for the signs indicating the seal preservation area, and what to do if one comes swimming by—essentially, look but don't touch.

⑦ James Joyce Museum. James Joyce wrote part of *Ulysses* in this sturdy, forbidding building, looking out to sea at Sandycove. The book's central character, Ulysses Bloom, wakes up here in the opening chapters, and the museum has been decked out to resemble the description from the book (with a few wry touches, such as a ceramic panther—representing the ferocious animal that appears to Bloom's roommate, Haines, in a dream). The building itself is a Martello tower, a small defensive fortification built by the British to ward off a feared invasion from France in the early 19th century. ⏱ *40 min. Joyce Tower, Sandycove.* ☎ *01-280 9265. Free admission. Daily 10am–4pm.*

8 ★ Bullock Castle & Harbour. Now owned by the Carmelite Sisters, the castle was once inhabited by monks who charged fishermen a quota of the fish they caught on the open seas. Without payment, they wouldn't be allowed back in the harbor. These days tiny Bullock Harbour is home to a colony of tame seals, who can often be seen bobbing between fishing boats.

9 ★ Dalkey Castle & Heritage Centre. Housed in a 15th-century tower house, this center tells the history of venerable Dalkey town in a few sweet, if unsophisticated, displays. Tours run by costumed guides tell the tale of the building (complete with live performance); or you can duck out of the tour and take in the view from the battlements instead. Adjoining the center is a medieval graveyard and the Church of St. Begnet (Dalkey's patron saint), whose foundations date back to Ireland's early Christian period. Dalkey itself is worth a wander; this heritage town has plenty of historic buildings, plus lots of charming pubs, restaurants,

Guides dressed up at Dalkey Castle.

and pricey little boutiques. If you enjoy country walks, climb Dalkey Hill in Dalkey Hill Park, just south of town, for great views of Killiney Bay, Bray Head, and Sugarloaf Mountain. ⏱ 1 hr. Castle St., Dalkey. www.dalkeycastle.com. ☎ 01-285 8366. Admission €8.50 adults, €7 seniors & students, €6.50 children aged 5–12 (children 4 & under free), €25 families. Mon, Wed–Fri 10am–5pm; Sat–Sun 11am–5pm.

Sandycove.

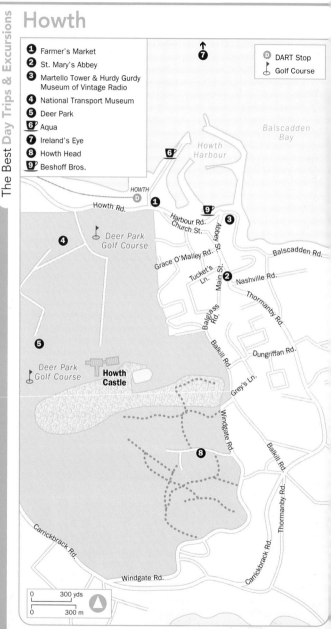

Howth

1 Farmer's Market
2 St. Mary's Abbey
3 Martello Tower & Hurdy Gurdy Museum of Vintage Radio
4 National Transport Museum
5 Deer Park
6 Aqua
7 Ireland's Eye
8 Howth Head
9 Beshoff Bros.

D DART Stop
⛳ Golf Course

Balscadden Bay

Howth Harbour

HOWTH

Howth Rd.

Harbour Rd.
Church St.

Abbey St.

Balscadden Rd.

Grace O'Malley Rd.

Tucket's Ln.

Main St.

Nashville Rd.

Thormanby Rd.

Deer Park Golf Course

Baliglass Rd.

Balkill Rd.

Dungriffan Rd.

Grey's Ln.

Deer Park Golf Course

Howth Castle

Windgate Rd.

Balkill Rd.

Thormanby Rd.

Carrickbrack Rd.

Carrickbrack Rd.

Windgate Rd.

0   300 yds
0   300 m

Relaxing Howth is loved for its coastal walks, plus trips to the tiny Ireland's Eye, and a museum housing historic fire engines. Located on the scenic Howth Peninsula, and once an island and sleepy fishing community, Howth is now a busy suburb and sprawling, prominent fishing center. START: **DART to Howth.**

Sea cliff walk at Howth.

❶ ★ **Farmer's Market.** Another busy open-air market, this one takes place along the seafront every Saturday, Sunday, and public holiday Monday. The market isn't huge—there are usually around 25 stalls here—but it has a great atmosphere, especially if the weather's good. There are usually stalls selling crafts and gifts, in addition to fresh cheeses, breads, and other tasty produce. *Harbour Rd. www. howthmarket.ie. Sat, Sun & public holiday Mon 10am–6pm.*

❷ ★★ **St. Mary's Abbey.** Take the steep uphill walk from the East Pier to the ruins of St. Mary's Abbey and graveyard, dating back to 1042. If nothing else, the view of the waterfront from here is superb. Dedicated to the Virgin Mary, this was a collegiate, indicating that it was served by a college or community of clerics who lived south of the church. It was first built in 1042 by King Sitric of Dublin, replaced in 1235 and again in the second half of the 14th century, and later modified. ⏱ *20 min.*

❸ ★★ **Martello Tower & Hurdy Gurdy Museum of Vintage Radio.** This charming and eccentric little museum was the work of a local enthusiast for all things vintage radio. It's packed to the gills with old radios, television sets, gramophones, and assorted golden-age ephemera. The museum is housed in another of the Martello towers that were built

Mini cupcakes at Howth Farmer's Market.

Ye Olde Hurdy Gurdy Museum of Vintage Radio.

along the coast in the early 19th century, to help fight off a French invasion that never happened. 🕐 *40 min. Martello Tower. https://sites.google.com/site/hurdygurdymuseum.* ☎ *086-815 4189. Admission: €5 adults, €3 students. Daily May–Oct 11am–4pm; Nov–Apr Sat–Sun 11am–4pm.*

④ ★ National Transport Museum. From one tightly packed museum to another. The National Transport Museum has around 60 lovingly preserved vehicles crammed in here—including trams, buses, fire engines, delivery trucks, and a host of other vintage

St. Mary's Abbey.

specimens, dating from the late 1800s up to the 1980s. (There isn't room to show everything, so the collection is regularly rotated.) Prized items include a "Merryweather" steam-driven fire engine from 1889. 🕐 *40 min. Heritage Depot, Howth Demesne. www.nationaltransportmuseum.org.* ☎ *01-832 0427. Admission: €4 adults, €3 seniors, students & children, €9.50 families. Sat–Sun & public holiday Mon 2–5pm. Bus: 31.*

⑤ ★ Deer Park. The walk from the Transport Museum takes you through the tranquil Deer Park (although deer remain elusive) past Howth Castle, dating back to 1450. The castle itself has now been converted into upmarket residences and is not open for public viewing. The **Rhododendron Gardens,** one of Europe's largest, lie a little deeper inside the park, and visitors in May and early June can gaze at the 40 varieties of glorious blooms in reds, pinks, and purples.

⑥ Aqua. One of the best restaurants in the area, Aqua has a commanding view from the West Pier. Lunch service is surprisingly affordable. *1 West Pier.* ☎ *01-832 0690. $*

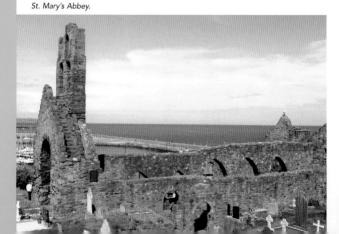

Ireland's Eye.

❼ ★★ Ireland's Eye. Boats leave regularly during the summer for the tiny island just 2km (1.2 miles) from Howth Harbour. This rocky outcrop is perfect for keen ornithologists and lovers of desolate beaches, dramatic cliffs, and ruined churches. It houses a Martello tower built in the early 19th century and the remains of a 6th-century monastic church, part of Howth's long Christian history. It is believed that the *Garland of Howth*, a Latin manuscript of the New Testament, now in Trinity College Library, was written here. Get out the binoculars to spot puffins, kittiwakes, and cormorants, and of course seals. Tread carefully (so you don't stand on eggs) and wander the island. It's hard to believe you're so close to the city. ○ *1½ hr. Boats run from East Pier. www.islandferries.net.* ☎ *086-845 9154. Fare €15 adults, €10 children, €40—€50 families (2 adults, 2 or 3 children). Call to check times. Approx. June–Aug daily 11am–6pm; Apr, Sept Sat–Sun 11am–6pm. Sailings at other times of year according to demand; phone to book. No fixed timings; boats leave approx every 30 min; journey takes 15 min.*

Practical Matters: Howth

Catch the DART 15km (9 miles) east to Howth, from city center stations including Connolly Station, Tara Street, Pearse, and Grand Canal Dock. Single tickets cost €2.30. Services run approximately every 20 to 30 minutes Monday to Saturday (7am–12:45pm) and every 20 to 40 minutes Sunday (9:30am–11:30pm). Round-trip tickets cost €6.15. Bus nos. 31 and 31B run from the city center, including Connolly Station. The Nitelink 31N night bus travels between Howth and Dublin city center every hour (Fri and Sat nights only). **Howth Tourism Information Office:** Ground Floor, 10 Harbour Rd., Howth. www.howthismagic.com. ☎ 01-840-0077.

National Transport Museum of Ireland.

8 ★★ Howth Head. If weather permits and you have enough time (it's no fun if it's too cloudy to see the view), take a walk along the Howth Peninsula coastline, passing the rugged landscape. Its summit is the perfect point to see the peninsula, with the Dublin Mountains in the background. There is a well-marked 7km (4.5-mile) path and large map at East Pier, or take the cliffside walk. All paths are well trodden, so take whichever one you fancy. Take a picnic to Howth Head for a dining experience with a spectacular view. ⏱ *2 hr.*

9 Beshoff Bros. This excellent fish and chips shop is a favorite with locals. There's no seating inside, so head over to the pier if weather permits—the view is simply wonderful. *12 Harbour Rd.* ☎ *01-832 1754. $.* ●

Before You Go

The Best Times to Go

May to September is the busiest time to visit, with myriad festivals throughout the summer, although it's also the time when you're least likely to snag an inexpensive hotel room. The months of May and September are often good choices, since your visit doesn't clash with the school summer vacation period. Hotels are invariably cheaper from **November to February.** There's no particular month to avoid, although be prepared for huge crowds in **March** for the St. Patrick's Day celebrations, a public holiday. The **Christmas** season sees shopping areas packed in the build-up, with special holiday markets opening. It's also a popular destination for **New Year's Eve,** especially to hear the midnight bells peal from Christ Church Cathedral, and see the New Year's Day parade. As Ireland's capital and a base to explore the country, Dublin enjoys year-round tourism plus major sporting events, so mid- to high-range hotels should be booked well in advance.

The Weather

With a cool, damp climate pretty much year-round, Dublin is not the place to come for a suntan. The warmest months are June to August, the likeliest time to enjoy sunny spells. In the event of a hot spell, most hotels have air-conditioning, if not a fan.

It's important to remember that it can rain at any time; be prepared for it, bring waterproofs, and take on the local cheerful attitude towards the odd shower, treating a sunny day and clear skies as a bonus. After all, this is what makes Ireland as green as it is.

The nights draw in early, and winter sets in, from November to February, although the temperature rarely falls to freezing.

Cellphones (Mobiles)

Before you leave your home country, check directly with your mobile phone provider to get the details on using your phone overseas. You may have to ask for the "international roaming" capability to be switched on—and that can't usually happen if you're already overseas.

Unfortunately, using your own phone in Ireland could prove very expensive. Most mobile phone companies charge very large premiums on call charges made while abroad. If you use a smartphone such as an iPhone or Android

DUBLIN AVERAGE TEMPERATURE & RAINFALL:

	JAN	FEB	MAR	APR	MAY	JUN
Daily temp (°F)	39	41	45	46	50	55
Daily temp (°C)	4	5	7	8	10	13
Rainfall (inch)	2.7	2.2	2.0	1.8	2.4	2.2
Rainfall (cm)	6.8	5.5	5.1	4.6	6.1	5.7

	JUL	AUG	SEP	OCT	NOV	DEC
Daily temp (°F)	59	59	55	50	45	43
Daily temp (°C)	15	15	13	10	7	6
Rainfall (inch)	2.7	2.8	2.8	2.8	2.7	2.8
Rainfall (cm)	6.9	7.2	7.1	7.0	6.8	7.0

Previous page: Dublin Bus.

Useful Websites

www.visitdublin.com: The official site of the **Dublin Tourist Office,** with maps, sightseeing, events, accommodation offers, and info on local transport.

www.discoverireland.com: Official site of **Tourism Ireland,** with information on the entire country, details on airlines flying into Dublin, and golf packages.

www.dublinks.com: Decent guide to events, sightseeing, and nightlife.

www.indublin.ie: Listings of events, comedy, music, theater, and reviews of bars and restaurants.

www.independent.ie: The online version of the daily Irish **Independent** newspaper with local and national news and events.

www.dublinbus.ie: Timetables, ticket info, and sightseeing tours for **Dublin Bus**.

www.irishrail.ie: Rail information to get around Ireland, plus **DART** timetables.

www.tickets.ie: Booking site for tickets for major events, with collection points around the city.

www.118.ie: Directory including shops, offices, and services from acupuncture to zip fasteners.

device, be sure to turn off features such as location services and push notifications, or you could end up facing *enormous* charges for data roaming. Similarly, you should always use Wi-Fi if you need to download anything.

To avoid all of this hassle, some travelers prefer to **rent** a phone for their trip to Ireland. You can do this from any number of overseas sites; several Irish phone companies have kiosks at the main airports, and car-rental agencies can usually rent you a phone for the duration of your stay. Alternatively, the company **Rent-a-Phone Ireland** (www.cell-phone-ireland.com; ☎ **087-683 4563**) enables you to reserve a phone in advance and pick it up from the arrivals lounge at Dublin airport. They charge around €80 per week for a standard phone (including €5 worth of calls—enough for

roughly a half-hour call to North America) or €100 for a smartphone, including €20 of calls and a 150MB data allowance. Rates drop for subsequent weeks.

Another option is to purchase a disposable "pay as you go" phone. Disposable phones aren't quite as big here as in some countries, due to the relatively low cost of phone contracts; however, you can buy them quite cheaply from mobile phone stores (most airports and almost any town of reasonable size will have at least one) or even some supermarkets.

Call charges in Ireland, and across the European Union, are much lower than they are in many other parts of the world, including the U.S; on pay-as-you-go, expect to pay around €0.35 per minute. You are not charged for incoming calls.

Car Rentals

Driving within Dublin is neither advised nor necessary, given the expensive parking, dreadful traffic jams, relatively cheap taxis, and decent bus service. Should you wish to drive farther afield, for example to explore Kildare, Wicklow, or Hill of Tara, it's better to book ahead with a car rental agency. Those with desks at the Dublin airport include **Avis** (www.avis.ie; ☎ **01-605 7500**); **Budget** (www.budget.ie; ☎ **01-844 5150**); **Enterprise** (www. enterprise.ie; ☎ **01-460 5042**); **Europcar** (www.europcar.ie; ☎ **01-812 2800**); and **Hertz** (www.hertz.ie; ☎ **01-844 5466**).

Getting There

By Plane

Dublin International Airport

(☎ www.dublinairport.com; 01/814-1111) is 11km (6¾ miles) north of the city center. A travel information desk in the arrivals concourse provides information on public bus and rail services throughout the country.

Aer Lingus (www.aerlingus.com; ☎ **081/836-5000**), Ireland's national airline, operates regular, direct scheduled flights between Dublin International Airport and numerous cities worldwide.

From the United States, direct routes include Boston, Chicago (O'Hare), New York (JFK), Orlando, and San Francisco. **American Airlines** (www.aa.com; ☎ **1800/433-7300**), **Delta** (www.delta.com; ☎ **1800/241-4141**), and **United** (www.united.com; ☎ **1800/864-8331**) all fly direct to Dublin from at least one of those same cities.

From Canada, direct flights are operated by **Air Canada** (www.air canada.com; ☎ **1888/247-2262**).

By Car

If you are arriving by car from other parts of Ireland or on a car ferry from Britain, all main roads lead into the heart of Dublin and are well signposted to **An Lar** (City Centre). The quickest way into Dublin from the airport is to take the Dublin Tunnel. The toll for cars is €3, or €10 between the hours of 6am and 10am Monday to Friday. To bypass the city center, the East Link toll bridge (€2) and West Link are signposted, and M50 circuits the city on three sides. From Wexford Town, Galway, or Belfast, the drive takes around 2 hours; from Cork, 2½ hours.

By Train

Called Iarnród Éireann in Gaelic, **Irish Rail** (www.irishrail.ie; ☎ 1890/778 899 for timetables, ☎ 1850-366-222 to prebook tickets) operates daily train service to Dublin from Belfast, Northern Ireland, and all major cities in the Irish Republic, including Cork, Galway, Limerick, Killarney, Sligo, Wexford, and Waterford. Trains from the south, west, and southwest arrive at Heuston Station, Kingsbridge, off St. John's Road; from the north and northwest at Connolly Station, Amiens Street; and from the southeast at Pearse Station, Westland Row, Tara Street.

By Ferry

Passenger and car ferries from Britain arrive at the Dublin Ferryport, on the eastern end of the North Docks. (In 2015 the regular ferry service between Dún Laoghaire and Holyhead in the U.K. ended after

204 years, so this is now the only option.) Contact **Irish Ferries** (www. irishferries.ie; ☎ **081-830 0400**); **P&O Irish Sea** (www.poirishsea. com; ☎ **087-166 6464** from the U.K); or **Stena Line** (www.stenaline.

com; ☎ **01-204 7777**) for bookings and information. Irish Ferries also sails to Dublin from Cherbourg in northern France. Buses and taxis serve both ports.

Getting **Around**

By Bus

After walking, buses are the most convenient and practical way to get between the city center sights. **Dublin Bus** operates a fleet of double-deckers, single-deckers, and minibuses (the latter charmingly called "imps"). Most originate on or near O'Connell Street, Abbey Street, and Eden Quay on the Northside, and at Aston Quay, College Street, and Fleet Street on the south side. Look for bus-stop markers resembling big blue or green lollipops—they're every few blocks on main thoroughfares. To tell where a bus is going, look at the destination street and bus number displayed above its front window; those heading for the city center indicate that with an odd mix of Latin and Gaelic: VIA AN LAR.

Bus service runs daily throughout the city, starting at 6am (10am on Sun), with the last bus at about 11:30pm.

On Friday and Saturday nights, **Nitelink** service runs from the city center to the suburbs from midnight to 4am. Buses operate every 30 minutes for most runs; schedules are posted on revolving notice boards at bus stops.

Inner-city fares are based on distances traveled. Daytime journeys that take place entirely within the designated "City Centre Zone" cost €0.70. This stretches from Parnell Square in the north, to Connolly Station and Merrion Square in

the east, St. Stephen's Green in the south, and Ormond Quay in the west. Longer journeys cost anything from €1.75 all the way up to around €5 if you're going as far as the outer suburbs.

You pay on board the bus, using an automatic fare machine located in front of the driver. **No Dublin bus accepts notes or gives change.** If you don't have the exact money in coins, the driver will issue you with a "change receipt." You must then take this to the Dublin Bus headquarters on O'Connell Street to collect your change (a process not designed to encourage refunds). The sole exception to this rule is route 747 ("Airlink"), which runs between the airport and the city center. It normally accepts notes and gives change.

By Tram

The sleek, modern (and wheelchair accessible) light rail tram system known as **Luas** runs from around 5:30am to 12:30am Monday to Friday, 6:30am to 12:30am Saturday, and 7am to 11:30pm on Sunday. (The last trams to certain stations are earlier—be sure to check the timetable.) There are two lines, Red and Green: The Green Line runs southeast from St. Stephen's Green to Sandyford in the south; the Red Line runs west from the Point, near the 3Arena in Dublin Docklands, to Connolly Railway Station, and swings down to the southwestern

Social Media

Users of social media, particularly Twitter, are uniquely placed to absorb a sense of what modern-day Ireland is really like through the eyes of its journalists, thinkers—and just ordinary folk with something to say. A few good Irish accounts to start with include **Frank Fitzgibbon** (@FrankSunTimes), editor of the Irish *Sunday Times;* **Niall Horan** (@NiallOfficial), the Irish contingent in the band One Direction (and, with over 24 million followers, Twitter royalty); the delightful and funny author **Marian Keyes** (@MarianKeyes); **Colm Tóibín** (@colmtobin), a writer with bone-dry wit, who just happens to share the name of a famous author; **Panti Bliss** (@Pantibliss), a Dublin drag queen who has recently found fame as an activist; **Amy Huberman** (@amyhuberman), an actress and Twitter natural who describes herself as "10% exhausted, 10% feared and 80% chocolate"; and radio presenter **Louise McSharry** (@louisemcsharry), known for discovering some of the best hottest talents in Irish music.

suburbs of Saggart and Tallaght. For further information, contact Luas (www.luas.ie; ☎ **1850/300-604**). The Luas network is currently undergoing long-term expansion work, which will extend the lines farther into the suburbs, with a projected completion date of late 2017. Until then, construction and roadworks are making Dublin's already chronic traffic problems worse—so, as the long-suffering locals will tell you, disruption is to be expected.

By DART

An acronym for Dublin Area Rapid Transit, the electric DART trains travel aboveground, linking the city center stations at **Connolly Station, Tara Street,** and **Pearse Street** with suburbs and seaside communities as far as Malahide to the north and Greystones to the south. Service operates roughly every 10 to 20 minutes Monday to Saturday from around 6am to midnight and Sunday from 9:30am to 11pm. For

further information, contact DART, Dublin Pearse Station (www.dart.ie; ☎ **1850/366-222**).

By Taxi

It can be difficult to hail a taxi on the street; however, you'll find them lined up at taxi stands (called "ranks") outside major hotels, at bus and train stations, and on prime thoroughfares such as Upper O'Connell Street, College Green, and the north side of St. Stephen's Green. You can also phone for a taxi; see the numbers listed in the "Fast Facts" section below.

On Foot

Marvelously compact, Dublin is ideal for walking. Just remember to look right and then left (and in the direction opposite your instincts if you're from North America) before crossing the street. Pedestrians have the right of way at specially marked, zebra-striped crossings (these intersections usually have two flashing lights).

Leap Cards

If you're likely to use public transport a lot while in Dublin (which we highly recommend), do as the locals do: Get a **Leap Card,** a prepaid card for reduced-cost travel on all Dublin buses (including Airlink and Nightlink), DART, Luas, and commuter trains. You can buy them at around 400 shops in and around the city—look for the distinctive green logo depicting a somewhat overexcited frog in mid-leap. (In Dublin Airport, you can pick one up at the small **Easons, Kiosk,** and **Spa** shops.) Ticket machines in some city-center DART and railway stations also dispense Leap Cards, or you can order them online at **www.leapcard.ie.** They're free, but you'll have to pay a refundable deposit of €5 adults, €3 children, and buy at least €5 worth of credit upfront.

Fast **Facts**

BUSINESS HOURS **Banks** are generally open 10am to 4pm Monday to Wednesday and Friday and 10am to 5pm on Thursday. **Post offices** (also known as An Post) are generally open from 9am to 5:30pm Monday to Friday and 9am to 1:30pm on Saturday. Some take an hour for lunch from 1 to 2pm, and small or rural branches may close on Saturday. **Museums and sights** are generally open 10am to 5pm Tuesday to Saturday and 2 to 5pm on Sunday. **Shops** generally open 9am to 6pm Monday to Saturday with late opening on Thursday until 7 or 8pm. Most shops in larger towns and cities will also open on Sundays (typically from late morning to late afternoon). Major shops, such as department stores, often stay open much later than other businesses

CONSULATES & EMBASSIES The **American Embassy** is at 42 Elgin Rd., Ballsbridge, Dublin 4 (dublin.usembassy.gov; ☎ **01/668-8777**); the **Canadian Embassy** is at 7–8 Wilton Terrace, Third Floor, Dublin 2 (www.canadainternational.gc.ca/ireland-irlande; ☎ **01/234-4000**); the **British Embassy** is at 29 Merrion Rd., Dublin 2 (www.gov.uk/government/world/organisations/british-embassy-dublin; ☎ **01/205-3700**); and the **Australian Embassy** is at Fitzwilton House, Seventh Floor, Wilton Terrace, Dublin 2 (www.ireland.embassy.gov.au; ☎ **01/664-5300**). In Northern Ireland, there's an **American Consulate** at Danesfort House, 223 Stranmillis Rd., Belfast BT9 5GR (belfast.usconsulate.gov; ☎ **028/9038-6100**).

DENTISTS For dental emergencies, your hotel will usually contact a dentist for you; otherwise, try **Smiles Dental Spa,** 28 O'Connell St. (☎ **1850/323-323**), or **Molesworth Dental Surgery,** 2 Molesworth Place (☎ **01/661-5544**).

DISABLED TRAVELERS For disabled travelers, Ireland is a mixed bag. Its modern buildings and cities are generally accessible, but many other buildings are historic, and those often lack wheelchair access. Trains can be accessed by wheelchairs but only with assistance. If you plan to travel by train in Ireland, be sure to check out **Iarnród Éireann's website** (www.irishrail.ie), which includes services for travelers with disabilities.

Finding accessible lodging can be tricky in Ireland. Many of the buildings here are hundreds of years old, and older hotels, small guesthouses, and landmark buildings still have steps outside and in. The rule of thumb should be: Never assume that a B&B, hotel, or restaurant has accessible facilities, and ask about your requirements before booking. Where there are serious mobility issues with a property, we've tried to mention them in this book. Equally, where they provide notably good facilities for travelers with disabilities, we've noted that too.

To research Ireland's accessibility options prior to your trip, one excellent online resource is **www.disability.ie.** For advice on travel to Northern Ireland, contact **Disability Action** (www.disabilityaction.org; ☎ **028/9029-7880**). The Northern Ireland Tourist Board also publishes a helpful annual *Information Guide to Accessible Accommodation,* available from any of its offices worldwide.

DOCTORS   For emergencies, dial ☎ **999.** If you need a doctor, your hotel should be able to contact one for you. Otherwise you could try **Dame Street Medical Center,** 16 Dame St. (☎ **01/679-0754**), or the **Suffolk Street Surgery,** 107 Grafton St. (☎ **01/679-8181**).

ELECTRICITY   Most hotels operate on 230 volts AC (50 cycles), three-pin plugs. Adaptors can be provided at major hotels.

EMERGENCIES   Dial ☎ **999** for police, ambulance, or fire emergencies.

GAY & LESBIAN TRAVELERS   Ireland has come a long way since homosexuality was legalized in 1993 (1982 in the North), but gay and lesbian visitors should be aware that this is still a conservative country. Cities like Dublin and Galway are far more liberal in their attitudes (particularly among the younger generation), and discrimination on the basis of sexuality is illegal throughout Ireland. Nonetheless, you should definitely proceed with caution when traveling in rural areas. Recommended websites for gay and lesbian travelers include **Gay Ireland** (www.gay-ireland.com) and **Outhouse** (www.outhouse.ie).

INTERNET   Wi-Fi is widespread in Irish hotels and B&Bs, even in rural areas. It's not universal, however. Most B&Bs and smaller hotels provide it for free, but larger hotels sometimes charge for access.

LANGUAGE   Ireland has two official languages—English and Gaelic—although in Dublin everyone speaks English. All signs in state-run public places (stations, street names, etc.) are legally required to be in Gaelic also. Look out for signs on the toilets—*Mna* actually means "women"!

LUGGAGE STORAGE   If you arrive at your hotel too early to check in, or if checkout is in the morning and your flight isn't until the evening, many hotels will watch your baggage for you. Alternatively, the **tourism office** (☎ **01/410-0700**) at 37 College Green, opposite Trinity College, can store bags securely for €5 per 24 hours. There's also a "Left Luggage" facility at the Terminal 1 parking lot at Dublin Airport.

LOST PROPERTY   If your passport is lost or stolen, contact your country's embassy immediately. Be sure to tell all of your credit card companies the minute you discover that your wallet is gone and file a report at the nearest police station.

MAIL & POSTAGE   In Ireland, mailboxes are painted green with the word POST on top. An airmail letter or postcard to any other country outside Europe, not exceeding 50 grams, costs €1.05.

MONEY   The Republic of Ireland uses the single European currency known as the **euro** (€). Euro notes come in denominations of €5, €10, €20, €50, €100, €200, and €500. The euro is divided into 100 cents; coins come in denominations of €2, €1, 50¢, 20¢, 10¢, 5¢, 2¢, and 1¢.

PASSPORTS No visas are required for U.S., U.K., Canadian, Australian, or New Zealand visitors to Ireland, for stays of up to 90 days. If your passport is lost or stolen, contact your country's embassy or consulate immediately (see Consulates & Embassies, p 169). Make a copy of your passport's critical pages before you leave and keep it in a safe place.

PHARMACIES Dublin does not have 24-hr. pharmacies. **City Pharmacy,** 14 Dame St. (☎ 01/670-4523), stays open until 9pm weekdays, 7pm Sat; **Boots the Chemist,** 20 Henry St. (☎ 01/873-0209), stays open until 9pm on Thursday, 8pm on Friday, 6pm Sunday, and 7pm all other days. There are also branches of Boots at 12 Grafton St. (☎ 01/677-3000) and in the **St. Stephen's Green Centre** (☎ 01/478-4368), but not all branches keep the same hours.

POLICE The national **police (Garda)** emergency number is ☎ **999** or ☎ **112.** Local police stations in the city include **Pearse Street** (☎ 01/666-9000) and **Store Street** (☎ 01/666-8000).

SAFETY By U.S. standards, Ireland is very safe, but particularly in the cities, it's not safe enough to warrant carelessness. Take the usual precautions in major cities: Watch your bags and valuables in busy places and keep cash and wallets out of sight; avoid walking in dark, quiet areas alone at night, including Phoenix Park; shield your PIN and take the cash away quickly from the ATM; keep money out of your back pocket. Most crime is drink- or drug-related, with drunken revelers a common sight in the city center

at weekends. If in doubt, avoid crowds like these. Drug dealers have been known to hang around the Liffey Boardwalk; look confident and don't make eye contact.

SENIOR TRAVEL In Ireland, seniors are sometimes referred to as "O.A.P.'s" (short for "Old Age Pensioners"). People over the age of 60 often qualify for reduced admission to museums and other attractions. Always ask about an O.A.P. discount if special rates are not posted. **Discover Ireland** can offer advice on how to find the best discounts.

SMOKING Smoking is banned on all public transport and in other public places. Pubs, clubs, and restaurants often have outside spaces and terraces for smokers.

TAXES As in many European countries, sales tax is VAT (value-added tax) and is often already included in the price quoted to you or shown on price tags. In the Republic, VAT rates vary—for hotels, restaurants, and car rentals, it is 13½%; for souvenirs and gifts, it is 23%. In Northern Ireland, the VAT is 20% across the board. VAT charged on services such as hotel stays, meals, car rentals, and entertainment cannot be refunded to visitors, but the VAT on products such as souvenirs is refundable. Save your receipts and present them at the Global Refund Desk when you get to the airport (they're located airside in the main terminal at Dublin; the desk is now an automated kiosk, located on the left just after you pass the Starbucks on the way to the departure gates). They can usually issue you a refund there and then. Some larger stores can issue you a Global Refund form and refund your VAT themselves, although you'll need to know your passport number, flight number, and departure time. In practice, this is usually much more fuss than it's worth.

TELEPHONES   For national directory inquiries, ☎ **11811;** for international ☎ **11818.** Telephone boxes dot the city, either coin-operated or with prepaid phonecards (available from newsagents and post offices). **Overseas calls** from Ireland can be quite costly, whether you use a local phone card or your own calling card.

To call Ireland from home:

1. **Dial the international access code:** 011 from the U.S., 00 from the U.K., 0011 from Australia, or 0170 from New Zealand.

2. **Dial the country code:** 353 for the Republic, 44 for the North.

3. **Dial the local number,** remembering to omit the initial 0, which is for use only within Ireland.

To make international calls from Ireland: First dial 00, then the country code (U.S. or Canada 1, U.K. 44, Australia 61, New Zealand 64). Next you dial the area code and local number. For example, to call the U.S. number 212/000-0000 you'd dial ☎ 00-1-212/000-0000. The toll-free international access code for AT&T is ☎ **1-800/550-000;** for Sprint it's ☎ **1-800/552001;** and for MCI it's ☎ **1-800/551-001.**

To make local calls: To dial a local number within the same area code, drop the initial 0. To dial a number within Ireland but in a different area code, use the initial 0.

TIME   Ireland follows Greenwich Mean Time from November to March, and British Summer Time from April to October. Ireland is 5 hours ahead of the eastern United States. Ireland's latitude makes for longer days and shorter nights in the summer and the reverse in the winter. In June, the sun doesn't fully set until around 11pm, but in December, it is dark by 4pm.

TIPPING   For taxi drivers, hairdressers, and other providers of service, tip an average of 10 to 15%. For restaurants, the policy is usually printed on the menu—either a gratuity of 10 to 15% is automatically added to your bill, or it's left up to you. As a rule, bartenders do not expect a tip, except when table service is provided.

TOILETS   Public bathrooms are usually simply called "toilets" or are marked with international symbols. In the Republic of Ireland, some of the older ones carry the Gaelic words FIR (men) and MNA (women). Check out malls and shopping centers for some of the newest and best-kept bathrooms in the country. Free restrooms are usually available to customers at sightseeing attractions, museums, hotels, restaurants, pubs, shops, and theaters. Many of the newer gas stations (called "petrol stations" in Ireland) have public toilets, and a few even have baby-changing facilities.

TOURIST INFORMATION   **Dublin Tourism** operates several walk-in visitor centers in greater Dublin that are open every day except Christmas. The principal center is on Suffolk Street, Dublin 2, open from Monday to Saturday from 9am to 5:30pm, Sunday and bank holidays 10:30am to 3pm. (It's easy to spot—just look for the rather racy statue of Molly Malone pushing her cart.) The Suffolk Street office has a currency exchange counter, a car-rental counter, an accommodation reservations service, bus and rail information desks, a gift shop, and a cafe. For accommodations reservations throughout Ireland by credit card (including some good last-minute deals on Dublin hotels), contact **Dublin Tourism** at **www. visitdublin.com** or ☎ **1890-324 583.** A tourism center is also in the Arrivals concourse of both terminals at Dublin Airport and at the ferry terminal at Dún Laoghaire Harbor.

WOMEN TRAVELERS Women should expect few, if any, problems traveling in Ireland. Women are accepted traveling alone or in groups in virtually every environment, and long gone are the days when women were expected to order half-pints of beer in pubs, while men were allowed to order the bigger, more cost-effective pints. In fact, the only time you're likely to attract any attention at all is if you eat alone in a restaurant at night—a sight that is still relatively uncommon in Ireland outside of the major cities. Even then, you'll not be hassled.

If you drink in a pub on your own, though, expect all kinds of attention, as a woman drinking alone is still considered to be "on the market"—even if she's reading a book, talking on her cellphone to her fiancé, or doing a crossword puzzle. So be prepared to fend them off. Irish men almost always respond well to polite rejection, though.

In cities, as ever, take a cab home at night and follow all the usual advice of caution you get when you travel anywhere. Essentially, don't do anything in Ireland that you wouldn't do at home

Dublin: **A Brief History**

600 B.C. The Celts first arrive in Ireland.

A.D. 432 St. Patrick arrives in Ireland and establishes the first Roman Catholic church—perhaps at the site of St. Patrick's Cathedral—and converts the Irish.

837 The Vikings arrive in Dublin, using the permanent settlement as a base to plunder surrounding regions.

1014 Brian Boru, high King of Ireland, defeats the Vikings at the battle of Clontarf.

1169 The Normans capture Dublin, led by Strongbow.

1541 Henry VIII is declared King of Ireland, and tries to introduce Protestantism.

1649 Oliver Cromwell's army lands in Dublin and then kills thousands in Drogheda. Land is taken from Catholic landowners and distributed around Cromwell's Protestant supporters.

1695 Penal laws restrict education for Catholics and prohibit them from buying property.

1727 Catholics deprived of the right to vote.

1759 Guinness Brewery is established in St. James's Gate.

1801 The Act of Union joins England to Ireland, prohibiting Catholics from holding public office.

1829 Daniel O'Connell, a Catholic lawyer, organizes the Catholic Association, helping to achieve the Catholic Emancipation Act.

1845–8 The Great Potato Famine: Over a million people die and more emigrate on America-bound boats from Dublin's docks.

1904 The Abbey Theatre opens.

1913 Jim Larkin, head of the Trade Union movement, leads the workers in the Great Lockout.

1914 Outbreak of World War I, delaying implementation of new Home Rule legislation.

1916 Nationalists stage Easter Rising, seizing the GPO and proclaiming an independent Irish Republic. The British crush the rising, and most of its leaders are executed.

1919–21 The Irish War of Independence against Britain; Eamon de Valera leads the nationalist movement Sinn Féin.

1920 British Parliament passes Government of Ireland Act, with one parliament for the six counties of Northern Ireland and one for the rest of Ireland.

1921 Anglo-Irish Treaty establishes the Irish Free State, partitioned from Northern Ireland.

1922 Dublin Parliament ratifies the treaty, leading to civil war between the IRA and Free State army, killing hundreds. Michael Collins assassinated.

1923 Irish Free State joins the League of Nations.

1926 De Valera founds the political party *Fianna Fáil.*

1932 Fianna Fáil wins General Election with de Valera head of government, and tries to eliminate British influence in Irish Free State.

1937 Fianna Fáil wins another election, and Irish Free State is abolished, proclaiming Eire (Gaelic for Ireland) as a sovereign state, with 32 counties.

1938 Douglas Hyde becomes first President of Eire; de Valera is first Prime Minister.

1939 Outbreak of World War II; Eire remains neutral but many Irish citizens join the Allied Forces.

1948 Fianna Fáil loses General Election; Dublin Parliament passes Republic of Ireland Bill.

1949 Easter Monday, anniversary of 1916 Uprising, Eire becomes Republic of Ireland and leaves the British Commonwealth.

1955 Ireland joins the United Nations, but refuses to join NATO because of Northern Ireland's status as part of the U.K.

1963 U.S. President John F. Kennedy visits Dublin.

1973 Ireland joins the European Economic Community (later known as the European Union).

1980S Dublin suffers the effects of severe economic problems, with high unemployment and rising debts. Many emigrate for better opportunities.

1985 Anglo-Irish Agreement is signed, giving Republic of Ireland a role in the government of Northern Ireland.

1986 Irish budget airline Ryanair's first flight from Dublin to London, quickly spreading routes to and from Europe and increasing tourism.

1990 Mary Robinson becomes first female President of Ireland.

1990S Dublin booms: Economic prosperity transforms Ireland (characterized as the Celtic Tiger) from one of Europe's poorest nations to one of its most successful. A time of immigration, rather than emigration.

1992 Ireland votes to loosen the strict abortion law, allowing travel abroad for an abortion.

1997 Divorce becomes legal in Ireland, although opposed by the Roman Catholic Church. The IRA declares a new cease-fire.

1998 Celebrations for the "Dublin Millennium," the date for the city's foundation having been decided upon as A.D. 998, when Norse King Glun Iariann agreed to pay taxes.

2002 The euro replaces the punt as Ireland's currency.

2004 Smoking is banned in all public places, including bars and restaurants. Publicans fear that this will lead to a drop in revenue.

2009 Ireland falls into "the worst recession in the developed world," according to the IMF, with more than 10% unemployment in Dublin.

2011 Queen Elizabeth pays an historic visit to Ireland, on the invitation of President Mary McAleese.

2015 A referendum to allow same-sex marriage passed by a landslide—making Ireland the first country in the world to pass such a law through a popular vote.

Dublin's **Architecture**

Medieval (12th–13th centuries A.D.)

Although the Vikings most certainly made their presence felt after their arrival in the 9th century, little remains of anything so early. In fact, most remains of the Viking settlement were only discovered during the "Battle of Wood Quay," when Dublin Corporation unearthed the site in the 1970s during excavation, but then insisted on building over it despite huge public pressure.

The grand **Christ Church Cathedral** existed from the Viking times, but was rebuilt by the Normans in the 12th century. The earliest sections surviving are the transept and the crypt, which extends the full length of the cathedral, and once contained three chapels. The Romanesque doorway on the south transept has intricate Irish stonework. Nearby **St. Patrick's Cathedral** was built in the 13th century but, again, has been constructed so many times that little remains of its medieval past, apart from the Romanesque door. Only the section of the choir gives a hint of the old style. **St. Audoen's Church** is Dublin's oldest surviving church, containing part of the original city wall. **St. Audoen's Arch,** in its grounds, is the last surviving entrance to the old city.

Post-Restoration (17th–18th centuries)

Ireland's first great classical building was **Royal Hospital Kilmainham,** inspired by the Hôtel des Invalides in Paris, designed by **William Robinson,** and now home to the Irish Museum of Modern Art. A huge quadrangle built around a courtyard, it has an arcade at ground level. Similar in style is the flat-fronted **Collins Barracks,** built in the early 18th century by **Thomas Burgh,** his first recorded building, with arcaded colonnades on two sides of the square. After the Royal Hospital, this was Dublin's earliest public building. Robinson then created the facade of the small but perfectly formed **Marsh's Library,** typical of a 17th-century scholar's library with decorative oak bookcases.

Georgian (18th century)

Dublin is best known for Georgian architecture, and its enduring image is of flat-fronted, brick houses with four- or five-floor terraces, usually planned around a private (as then) square. A time when the affluent Protestant gentry were only too happy to improve the city, it was the symmetry and harmony of classical architecture that formed the basis for this style. The **Gardiner** family was the most influential of the private developers, and laid out Parnell Square, Mountjoy Square, and Henrietta Street, which meant the north side was, for a short time, the city's most fashionable area. The city's town houses were brick-built with a basement and symmetrically arranged windows that got shorter higher up to give the illusion of greater height. The best examples today can be seen at **Merrion Square,** which these days is very much a *des res* area. The fanlights over the front doors, and how ornate they were, indicated the wealth and prestige of the owner. They may have looked unadorned from the outside, but plasterers *extraordinaires* enhanced everything, such as **La Franchini** brothers (Newman House).

In addition to the residential squares and terraces, the era was also marked by **James Gandon's Custom House** and the **Four Courts,** both on the Liffey's north bank. These grand buildings were built in the classical style with domes, ornate decoration, and symbolic sculpture adorning the gateways.

Notable architects of the time were German-born **Richard Cassels,** who worked on the **Houses of Parliament** and **Leinster House,** the latter built for the Earl of Kildare. **Sir Edward Lovett Pearce** is the main man behind Palladianism in Ireland, including the **Houses of Parliament** (now the Bank of Ireland).

Victorian (19th century)

Dublin suffered a decline following the Act of Union, so there are relatively few Victorian masterpieces around the city. But those that remain make their mark. The stunning redbrick **George's Street Arcade** was Dublin's first and only Victorian shopping center, with an ornate Gothic exterior. Traditional bars are the best way of seeing Victorian architecture and interior design; those with rarely changed Victorian interiors include **Ryan's** and the **Stag's Head,** all mahogany paneling and snugs to keep the drinking discrete.

Modern (20th century to present)

The most (in)famous new addition to Dublin's architectural scene is **The Spire,** causing mayhem when it was completed in 2002 to mark the new Millennium (late). The stainless-steel spire is 120m (366 ft.) high and the tallest structure in Dublin. Other slightly less controversial contemporary creations include the **IFSC,** the International Financial Services Centre, the modern-day powerhouse of Ireland's vibrant economy (in something of a downswing since the 2008 recession), and the first phase of the Dublin Corporation Offices by Sam Stephenson, one of Dublin's best-known contemporary architects. New creations around the docklands, among its sea of glass apartments, mainly empty, include **Grand Canal Square,** designed by **Martha Schwartz.** Within the square, **Grand Canal Theatre,** designed by another U.S. supremo architect Daniel Libeskind, opened in March 2010, and is loved for its angular-themed exterior in glass and steel.

Dublin in **Literature**

Ireland holds a place in literature disproportionate to its small size and modest population. Four writers from this tiny country have won the Nobel Prize for literature. Inspired by the country's unique beauty, the inequities of its political system, and its cruel legacy of poverty and struggle, Ireland's authors, poets, and playwrights write about the Irish for the Irish and to raise awareness in the rest of the world. No matter where you live, you've probably been reading about Ireland all your life.

Born in Dublin in 1854, **Oscar Wilde** was a popular and successful student at Trinity College, winning a scholarship to continue his studies in England at Oxford. After a flamboyant time there, he graduated with top honors and returned to Ireland, only to lose his girlfriend to Bram Stoker in 1878, after which he left Ireland forever. His writing—including the novel *The Picture of Dorian Gray*, plays including *The Importance of Being Earnest*, and books of poetry—were often overshadowed by his scandalous personal life. Although a statue of him stands in Dublin in **St. Stephen's Green ★** (p 30), his works were largely inspired by British and French writers, and he spent the majority of his life abroad.

George Bernard Shaw was born in Dublin in 1856 and attended school in the city but never went to college, as he came to loathe the organized education system. His literary style was, therefore, self-taught, and he spent his life studying and writing. He moved to England as a young man and lived much of his life in a village in Hertfordshire in England. As a result, many of his works have a distinctly English feel. His plays are known both for their sharp wit and for their sense of outrage over unfairness in society and the absurdity of the British class system. He is the only person ever to have won both the Nobel Prize and an Oscar (for *Pygmalion*).

James Joyce was born in the Dublin suburb of Rathgar in 1882 and educated at Jesuit boarding schools and later at Trinity College. He wrote vividly—and sometimes impenetrably—about Dublin, despite spending much of his life as an expat living nomadically in Europe. His controversial and hugely complex novels *Ulysses* and *Finnegan's Wake* are his most celebrated (and least understood) works. They and his collection of short stories, *Dubliners*, touch deeply on the character of the people of Dublin. The **James Joyce Centre ★** (p 26) is a mecca for Joyce fans.

The poet and playwright **Samuel Beckett** was born in 1906 in the Dublin suburb of Foxrock and educated at Trinity College. His work, however, was heavily influenced by German and French postmodernists, and he spent much of his life abroad, even serving with the Resistance in France during World War II. Best known for his complex absurdist play *Waiting for Godot*, he won the Nobel Prize in 1969.

The controversial writer, erstwhile terrorist, and all-round bon vivant **Brendan Behan** was born in Dublin in 1923. Behan came by his revolutionary fervor honestly: His father fought in the Easter Rising and his mother was a close friend of Michael Collins. When he was 14, Behan joined Fianna Éireann, the youth organization of the IRA. An incompetent terrorist, he was arrested on his first solo mission to blow up England's Liverpool Docks when he was 16 years old. His autobiographical book, *Borstal Boy*, describes this period in his life in exquisite detail. His play *The Quare Fellow* made him an international literary star, and he would spend the rest of his life as a jolly, hopeless alcoholic, drinking his way through London, Dublin, and New York, better known for his quick wit and bons mots than for his plays.

Among modern Irish writers, the best known is arguably the poet **Seamus Heaney,** born in 1939 near a small town called Castledawson in Northern Ireland. As a child he won scholarships to boarding school in Derry and later to Queen's University in Belfast. His years studying classic ancient Greek and Latin literature and Anglo-Saxon writing heavily influenced his poetry, but all of his writing is marked by his life in the troubled region where he grew up. His works, including *The Cure at Troy* (based on the works of Sophocles), *The Haw Lantern, The Government of the Tongue*, and a modern translation of *Beowulf*, ultimately earned him the Nobel Prize in 1995. Heaney's death in the summer of 2013 brought an outpouring of affection from fans across the world.

Other contemporary Irish writers include **Marian Keyes** (whose hugely popular novels include *Lucy Sullivan is Getting Married* and *This Charming Man*), **Roddy Doyle** (*The Commitments, Paddy Clarke Ha Ha Ha*), and the late **Maeve Binchy** (*A Week in Winter, Circle of Friends*).

Dublin in **Film**

Many aspects of life in the capital have been tackled by an international array of directors and actors. Here are a few of the better-known films to have prominently featured Dublin—and a few obscure gems worth seeking out.

The Commitments (directed by Alan Parker, 1991) may be the most famous Irish musical ever made. With its cast of young, largely inexperienced Irish actors playing musicians dedicated to American soul music, it's a delightful piece of filmmaking.

Intermission (directed by Jim Crowley, 2003) is a lively urban romance filmed on location in Dublin, featuring the Irish actor Colin Farrell (talking in his real accent for a change). It's a great look at Dublin right in the middle of its economic boom.

Veronica Guerin (directed by Joel Schumacher, 2003) is a dark, fact-based film (with the Australian actress Cate Blanchett doing an excellent Irish accent) about a troubled Irish investigative reporter on the trail of a drug boss.

Once (directed by John Carney, 2007) is a touching, Oscar-nominated portrait of two struggling young musicians—an Irish singer (played by the Irish actor/musician Glen Hansard) and a Czech piano player trying to make it big in Dublin. The film was subsequently turned into a hit stage musical.

Based on a popular TV sitcom, ***Mrs. Brown's Boys D'Movie*** (directed by Ben Kellett, 2014) is a broad, slapstick comedy about a no-nonsense Dublin matriarch. The film became one of the most successful Irish films of the decade at the box office, despite being almost universally derided as terrible by critics (spoiler alert: They're right). ●

Index

See also Accommodations and Restaurant indexes, below.

Photo **Credits**

p viii: © Rolf G Wackenberg/Shutterstock.com; p 3, bottom: © Fáilte Ireland/Andrew Bradley; p 4, top: © Sean Pavone; p 4, bottom: © Fáilte Ireland/Rob Durston; p 5: © David
Soanes; p 7, middle: © Shadowgate; p 7, bottom: © Tourism Ireland/James Fennell; p 8,
bottom: © Fáilte Ireland/Rob Durston; p 9, top: © Tourism Ireland/Tony Pleavin; p 9, bot-
tom: © Tourism Ireland/Brian Morrison; p 10, bottom: © DRTA; p 13, bottom: © Tourism
Ireland; p 14, top: © DRTA; p 15, bottom: © Tourism Ireland; p 16, bottom: © Tourism Ire-
land; p 17, top: © Tourism Ireland/Tony Pleavin; p 19, bottom: © Tourism Ireland/Tony
Pleavin; p 20, top: © Tourism Ireland/Brian Morrison; p 21, bottom: © Tourism Ireland/Chris
Hill Photographic; p 22, top: Courtesy of The Cobblestones; p 23: © Tourism Ireland/Brian
Morrison; p 25, bottom: © Tourism Ireland; p 26, bottom: © Tourism Ireland; p 27, top:
© Semmick Photo/Shutterstock.com; p 30, bottom: © Tourism Ireland/Tony Pleavin; p 31,
top: © William Murphy; p 32, top: © Tourism Ireland/Tony Pleavin; p 32, bottom: © Tour-
ism Ireland/Dublinia; p 33, bottom: © Sean MacEntee; p 35, middle: © Tourism Ireland/
Brian Morrison; p 36, bottom: © Tourism Ireland/Brian Morrison; p 39, bottom: © Tourism

Photo Credits

Ireland; p 40, bottom: © Fáilte Ireland/Rob Durston; p 41, top: © Fáilte Ireland/Rob Durston; p 41, bottom: © DRTA; p 42, bottom: © Eoin O'Mahony; p 45, bottom: © Tourism Ireland/Government of Ireland National Monuments Service Photographic Unit; p 46, bottom: © Leonid Andronov; p 48, top: © Fáilte Ireland/Rob Durston; p 49: © Tourism Ireland/James Fennell; p 51, bottom: © Tourism Ireland/Brian Morrison; p 52, bottom: © William Murphy; p 53, top: © DRTA; p 55, middle: © Tourism Ireland/Clara Hooper; p 55, bottom: © Fáilte Ireland/Tara Morgan; p 56, top: © Aitormmfoto; p 57, top: © Tourism Ireland; p 59, bottom: © Noel Moore/Shutterstock.com; p 60, top: © Jennifer Boyer; p 60, bottom: © Fáilte Ireland/Rob Durston; p 61, top: © DRTA; p 61, bottom: © Tourism Ireland; p 63, bottom: © Fáilte Ireland/Clara Hooper; p 64, top: © Fáilte Ireland/Andrew Bradley; p 64, bottom: © Semmick Photo/Shutterstock.com; p 65, top: © Fáilte Ireland ; p 67, bottom: © Carlos Luna; p 68, bottom: © Tourism Ireland/DAV; p 69, top: © Tourism Ireland; p 71, bottom: © Tourism Ireland/Brian Morrison; p 72, top: © Aitormmfoto/Shutterstock.com; p 72, bottom: © Tourism Ireland/Government of Ireland National Monuments Service Photographic Unit; p 73, top: © DRTA; p 74, top: © Fáilte Ireland/Rob Durston; p 74, bottom: © William Murphy; p 75: Courtesy of Om Diva; p 76, middle: Courtesy of Danker Antiques; p 80, bottom: Courtesy of The Doorway Gallery; p 81, top: Courtesy of Hodges Figgis/Tony Hayes; p 82, bottom: © Sebastian Dooris; p 83, top: © Fáilte Ireland/Rob Durston; p 83, bottom: © Fáilte Ireland/Andrew Bradley; p 85, top: Courtesy of Sheridan's Cheesemonger; p 85, bottom: © Avoca Ireland; p 86, top: © DRTA; p 86, bottom: Courtesy of the KEMP Gallery; p 87, top: Courtesy of Weir & Sons; p 87, bottom: © Tourism Ireland/iamacosmonaut; p 88, top: © Fáilte Ireland; p 89: © Rolf G Wackenberg/Shutterstock.com; p 91, bottom: © Brendan Howard/Shutterstock.com; p 92, bottom: © Fáilte Ireland/Rob Durston; p 93, bottom: © Fáilte Ireland/Rob Durston; p 95, bottom: © Victor Maschek/Shutterstock.com; p 96, bottom: © Tourism Ireland/Tony Pleavin; p 97, top: © Jurand; p 97, bottom: © LarryDJ; p 98, bottom: © Semmick Photo/Shutterstock.com; p 99: Courtesy of Super Miss Sue's/Terry Mcdonagh; p 102, middle: Courtesy of 101 Talbot; p 103, bottom: Courtesy of Avoca Ireland; p 104, bottom: Courtesy of Chapter One/Barbara Corsico; p 105, top: Courtesy of Aqua/Paul Sherwood ; p 106, bottom: Courtesy of Bang; p 107, top: Courtesy of Brasserie 6/Damian Bligh; p 108, bottom: © William Murphy; p 109, middle: Courtesy of San Lorenzo; p 110, top: Courtesy of The Vintage Kitchen; p 110, bottom: Courtesy of Super Miss Sue's/Terry Mcdonagh; p 111, top: Courtesy of Merry Ploughboy; p 111, bottom: Courtesy of Tourism Ireland; p 112, top: Courtesy of The Sussex; p 113: © Barnacles Budget Accommodation; p 116, middle: Courtesy of Fáilte Ireland/Gareth Byrne; p 117, bottom: © Chad and Steph; p 118, top: Courtesy of Bank/James Fennell; p 118, bottom: © DRTA; p 119, bottom: Courtesy of Fáilte Ireland; p 120, top: Courtesy of Tourism Ireland DAV; p 120, bottom: Courtesy of Cobblestones/Steve de Paoire ; p 121, top: Courtesy of Merry Ploughboy; p 121, bottom: © Irish Typepad; p 122, bottom: Courtesy of Lillies Bordello; p 123: © Fáilte Ireland; p 124, top: © DRTA; p 128, bottom: Courtesy of the Opera Theatre Company; p 129: Courtesy of Cineworld; p 130, top: © Caroline Delaney; p 130, bottom: Courtesy of Whelans/Dara Munnis; p 131, bottom: © Tourism Ireland/Jonathon Hessian; p 133, top: © DRTA; p 133, bottom: © Tourism Ireland/Matteo Tuniz; p 134, bottom: © Fáilte Ireland/Andrew Bradley; p 135: © Tourism Ireland; p 140, bottom: Courtesy of Ariel House; p 141, top: Courtesy of Ashling Hotel; p 142, top: Courtesy of Buswells; p 143, bottom: Courtesy of Camden Court Hotel; p 144, bottom: Courtesy of Grand Canal Hotel/Paul Sherwood ; p 145, bottom: Courtesy of Merchant House; p 146, bottom: Courtesy of Mespil Hotel; p 147, top: Courtesy of The Morrison; p 147, bottom: Courtesy of DRTA ; p 149: © Tourism Ireland/Brian Morrison; p 151, bottom: © Tourism Ireland ; p 152, top: © Tourism Ireland ; p 152, bottom: © Tourism Ireland/Brian Morrison; p 155, bottom: © Tourism Ireland/Jason Baxter; p 156, bottom: © Tourism Ireland/Jason Baxter; p 157, top: © Fáilte Ireland/Rob Durston; p 157, bottom: © Owen J Fitzpatrick/Shutterstock.com; p 159, middle: © Tourism Ireland/Brian Morrison; p 159, bottom: © Laura Planells; p 160, top: © William Murphy; p 160, bottom: © Matyas Rehak; p 161, top: © chripell; p 162, top: © Ana Rey; p 163: © Steeve Roche